THE GREAT AMERICAN THINKERS SERIES

The first twelve volumes in the series will be:

THOMAS JEFFERSON, by Stuart Gerry Brown, Ph.D., Maxwell Professor of American Civilization, Syracuse University.

JOHN C. CALHOUN, by Richard N. Current, Ph.D., Professor of History, University of Wisconsin.

CHAUNCEY WRIGHT, by Edward Madden, Ph.D., Professor of Philosophy, San Jose State College.

In preparation:

CHARLES PEIRCE, by Thomas S. Knight, Ph.D., Associate Professor of Philosophy, Utica College of Syracuse University.

THEODORE PARKER, by Arthur W. Brown, Ph.D., Director of the Institute of Humanities and Chairman of the English Department, Adelphi University.

WILLIAM JAMES, by Edward C. Moore, Ph.D., Graduate Dean and Coordinator of Research, University of Massachusetts.

JOHN WOOLMAN, by Edwin H. Cady, Ph.D., Rudy Professor of English, University of Indiana.

GEORGE BANCROFT, by Russel B. Nye, Ph.D., Professor of English, Michigan State University.

THORSTEIN VEBLEN, by Douglas Dowd, Ph.D., Associate Professor of Economics, Cornell University.

BENJAMIN FRANKLIN, by Ralph L. Ketcham, Ph.D., Associate Editor of the *Papers of Benjamin Franklin,* Yale University, and Professor of American Studies, Syracuse University.

JONATHAN EDWARDS, by Alfred Owen Aldridge, Ph.D., Professor of English and Director of the Program of Comparative Literature, University of Maryland.

JOHN DEWEY, by Richard J. Bernstein, Ph.D., Associate Professor of Philosophy, Yale University, and Assistant Editor of *Review of Metaphysics.*

CHAUNCEY WRIGHT

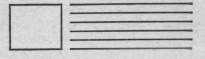

Author of this volume: Edward
H. Madden, Ph.D., Professor of
Philosophy, San Jose State College.

Series Editors: Thomas S. Knight,
Ph.D., Associate Professor of Phi-
losophy, Utica College of Syracuse
University; and Arthur W. Brown,
Ph.D., Director of the Institute of
Humanities and Chairman of the
English Department, Adelphi Uni-
versity.

WASHINGTON SQUARE PRESS, INC. • NEW YORK

CHAUNCEY WRIGHT

A *Washington Square Press* edition
1st printing....................February, 1964

L

Published by
Washington Square Press, Inc., 630 Fifth Avenue, New York, N.Y.

WASHINGTON SQUARE PRESS editions are distributed in
the U.S.A. by Affiliated Publishers, a division of Pocket
Books, Inc., 630 Fifth Avenue, New York 20, N.Y.

CONTENTS

1. Character and Background   1
  1. SOCRATES OF BOW STREET   2
  2. ADVOCATE OF EVOLUTION   12

2. Religion   20
  1. A RELIGIOUS SKEPTIC   20
  2. THE IMPORTANCE OF THERAPY   27
  3. IS THE SKEPTIC IRRELIGIOUS?   31
  4. A NON-THEISTIC COSMOLOGY   33

3. Morality   39
  1. MORALITY OR SKEPTICISM?   39
  2. THE GREATEST HAPPINESS PRINCIPLE   44
  3. PRACTICAL PROBLEMS   53

4. Science   59
  1. MISCONCEPTIONS   59
  2. EVOLUTION AND NATURAL SELECTION   67
  3. TWO KINDS OF EXPLANATION   72

5. Perennial Problems   79
  1. THE ROLE OF COMMON SENSE   79
  2. IS *a priori* KNOWLEDGE POSSIBLE?   81
  3. THE MEANING OF "CAUSE"   86
  4. THE NATURE OF SPACE   90

CONTENTS

6. Physical Objects   97
   1. THE OLD VIEWS   97
   2. THE NEW VIEW   103
   3. THE NOTION OF SUBSTANCE   109

7. Historical Bearings   115
   1. THE AMERICAN SCENE   115
   2. THE LARGER SCENE   121
   3. WRIGHT'S INFLUENCE   126

Notes   135

Annotated Bibliography   149

Index   165

Chapter 1

CHARACTER AND BACKGROUND

Chauncey Wright's life was simple and straightforward, though not always happily lived, and his philosophy was sophisticated and new, though not always felicitously phrased.[1] His greatness and his failure in both of these aspects are of almost equal interest.

The external events of Wright's life are easy to outline.[2] He was born in Northampton, Massachusetts, in 1830. After graduation from Harvard in 1852, he worked on the mathematics staff of the *Nautical Almanac* until 1870. In 1860 he was elected a fellow of the American Academy of Arts and Sciences, of which he was secretary for a while. He lectured at Harvard in philosophy and psychology in 1870 and in mathematical physics in 1874. A high spot in his life was his visit to Darwin in England in 1872. Between 1864 and 1875, when he died in Cambridge, he wrote many articles and reviews for the *Nation* and the *North American Review,* culturally two of the most important journals in nineteenth-century America. Charles Eliot Norton, Wright's closest friend in later years, published Wright's essays posthumously in 1877 under the title *Philosophical Discussions;* and James Bradley Thayer, his lifelong friend, published his *Letters* posthumously in 1878. These are the externals. They paradoxically both conceal and reveal a good deal about the existence and essence of Chauncey Wright. I shall try to relate their significance to Wright's ultimate accomplishments.

1. SOCRATES OF BOW STREET

Chauncey was the son of Ansel Wright, Northampton groceryman and deputy sheriff, and Elizabeth Boleyn, an unsmiling housewife. While Chauncey inherited his mother's sometimes shy and melancholy ways, he also caught from his father a never-failing sense of humor and consideration of others. His education was quite traditional until he had the good fortune to attend the Select High School in Northampton, where he came under the influence of David S. Sheldon, a scholarly and thoughtful person of unusual ability. Sheldon inspired Wright toward an interest in science and mathematics and introduced him to Robert Chambers' *Vestiges of the Natural History of Creation,* a widely read and thoroughly condemned defense of the evolutionary point of view.

While Wright was brilliant in science and mathematics, he was deficient in Latin and Greek grammar and received only a conditional admission to Harvard in 1848. That he went to college at all, and to Harvard specifically, was owing to the kindly interest of a staunch friend, Mrs. Ann Lyman.

In college the story of Wright's achievement was the same; he was a first-rate student of science and mathematics and slow in languages. His fame among fellow students was substantial, however, since he managed to arrive at original mathematical proofs in Professor Benjamin Peirce's class and happily saved the academic averages of his friends by tutoring. But they had to be his friends, for he was as shy as a hermit crab during the Harvard years and would scuttle off if a stranger happened to invade a friend's room. He showed some aptitude for philosophy, though nothing to suggest his later devotion to it. Since he already found his Christian background, liberal as it was, too spiritually confining, he was drawn particularly to Ralph Waldo Emerson's essays.[3]

After college Wright quietly acquired his most important education, wholly self-directed. He was interested in Francis Bacon and William Whewell, but the major influences were Sir William Hamilton, John Stuart Mill, and Charles Darwin. Slowly the influence of Hamilton was displaced by that of Mill and Darwin. While he studied philosophy, Wright earned his living by mathematical piecework for the *Nautical Almanac*. In a way this arrangement was ideal, for he invented new computational devices allowing him to do a year's work in three months, leaving the rest of the time for studying and talking philosophy with friends like J. B. Thayer, E. W. Gurney, who was later Dean of Harvard College, and a host of others.

Also during this early period Wright blossomed socially, taking a prominent part in discussions at Mrs. Charles Lowell's (James Russell Lowell's sister-in-law) and helping to found the Septem, a group of seven friends, all members of the Harvard classes of 1852 and 1853. The Septem met regularly for years to discuss papers on philosophical and political topics and to indulge in whatever festivities happened at the moment to recommend themselves.[4] Wright greatly enjoyed these festivities and began the excessive use of alcohol which caused him much trouble later in his life. He wrote Gurney a letter in which he jokingly empowered his friend to dispose of his person after the Club meetings, however friendship might dictate.[5] In later years his friends came to remember the occasions of such humor with sadness and a sense of despair.

For years Wright took his meals at the home of Mrs. Lyman, who had moved to Cambridge to be near her sisters. Mary Walker, an escaped Negro slave, loyally served Mrs. Lyman. To this little household on Garden Street Chauncey gave a stability which it badly needed; and Susan Lesley, Mrs. Lyman's daughter, to whom Chauncey was also devoted, deeply appreciated his steadying influence on these lonely women.[6] In the summer, when Susan and her daughter visited Mrs. Lyman, Chauncey gave long and loving care to little Mary. Children were invariably drawn to him and were fascinated by his never-ending stock of riddles, rhymes and games.

Yet in spite of appearances, all was not going well. He had greater difficulty each year in finishing his almanac work on time, and the three months at the end of the year became a kind of purgatory to him. He smoked and drank excessively. These habits, along with late hours of work and irregular eating, broke down his resistance. Moreover, his old friends were marrying one by one and were no longer available for Socratic sessions. Worse yet, the Lesleys had reluctantly placed Mrs. Lyman in an asylum, and Chauncey lost the only home he really had in Cambridge. In 1863 he developed a painful foot infection which would not heal properly. These accumulated ills drove Wright into a state of depression. His days seemed endlessly long. The dust grew thick on his books, but he could not have cared less.

He lost interest even in talking philosophy. His friends were dismayed and sought ways to help him.

His old friend Gurney and his new friend Charles Eliot Norton, with attentiveness and easy conversation, successfully roused him from despair. Most important for his recovery, he had found a home again. From 1864 on, Wright visited the Norton household daily, becoming a great favorite with the whole family, and especially with Norton's wife, Susan.

In the years from 1864 to 1869 Wright became a philosopher in his own right. His numerous articles and reviews in the *Nation* and the *North American Review* dealt most impressively with natural theology, the philosophy of Herbert Spencer, and a physical theory of the universe.[7] The Septem was revived; he could talk philosophy with Gurney and Norton to his heart's content; and he lived happily at the home of Mary Walker. He increased his circle of friends adding, among others, the Nortons' close friend, G. W. Curtis, political editor of *Harper's Weekly* and a "practical" transcendentalist.[8] Wright heard echoes of Emerson's voice in Curtis' talk and remembered pleasantly the enthusiasm for Emerson of his Harvard days.

Unhappily, though, the old trouble recurred in 1869. Irregular habits plus the loss of friends and loved ones were again responsible. The Septem again collapsed, Gurney married, and the Nortons went to Europe for several years. Wright gave up all his almanac work, dropped his clubs, and wrote and talked philosophy no longer.

He was in real trouble this time, for he had become chronically addicted to alcohol. His friends, saddened by his dreadful lethargy, again sought him out more often and engaged him in greater correspondence. But recovery came less quickly this time. He struggled only to fall back again. When this happened, however, a friend invariably was close at hand. Finally, after much effort on everyone's part, Wright was reclaimed from depression and resumed his old philosophical ways.

From 1870 to 1875 Wright wrote his most important philosophical articles and a series of philosophical letters to members of the Norton family. Fortunately, during these years, he never lacked a sympathetic audience for his Socratic searchings: he always had a group of bright young Harvard students and graduates who were tired of the Christian orthodoxy of the Divinity School and the philosophy department, and who preferred Wright's daring journeys into forbidden waters. To these years belongs the club which C. S. Peirce later called *his* Metaphysical Club,[9] although none of its other members recalled either that it was Peirce's or that it bore that name. Besides Wright, who was the acknowledged leader of the younger men, Peirce, William James, Oliver Wendell Holmes, Jr., Nicholas St. John Green, and occasionally John Fiske and Francis E. Abbot belonged to this group. Of Wright at this time, James wrote, ". . . he was not merely the great mind of a village—if Cambridge will pardon the expression—but either in London or Berlin he would, with equal ease, have taken the place of master which he held with us."[10]

In 1870 the Dean of Harvard College invited Wright to lecture on psychology and in 1874 on mathematical physics. The invitation, after all, was not too surprising since Gurney was the Dean. Moreover, Charles William Eliot, another member of the Septem, was the new President. These men respected

Wright's talents and hoped to make use of them permanently in the College. Wright was delighted with the opportunity to teach psychology, for it would give him ample opportunity to bring up philosophical topics. He viewed it as a chance to wage war against the Harvard philosophy department, consisting of Francis Bowen and Andrew Peabody, and the Harvard Divinity School—both of which, he felt, exemplified academic orthodoxy at its worst. "I may prevail against the hosts of the enemy, and put to rout the forces which Professor Bowen and Dr. Peabody and the Divinity School still continue to command for the subjugation of the human mind."[11] Unfortunately, however, the opposition would not listen. Bowen and Peabody never attended his lectures, and Dr. Stearns of the Divinity School after appearing once never returned.

Unhappily for Chauncey it was not only members of the philosophy department and the Divinity School who did not listen. The truth is he was not a teacher. He was terrified by a group of people hanging on his every word. He longed for a man who could ask questions and talk back. When no one responded, he spoke monotonously, looked blank, and fixed his eyes on his desk—appearing to the class to have his eyes shut. Apparently the class responded in a like manner. Wright just did not "have it in him" to be a Harvard professor.

Gurney and Eliot never lost faith in him, for in 1874 they asked him to teach a course in mathematical physics. Wright took on the course in the middle of the year from a professor who found his load too heavy, an unhappy way for anyone to begin teaching. He had ten clever sophomores in the course and thought things would go better. But it did not turn out that way. The students complained to Dean Gurney that Wright was too advanced for them to follow.

This failure was the end. He was not asked to return. Yet Wright's failure at Harvard is not at all surprising. Certainly Socrates in a classroom would have been an anomaly. He needed to buttonhole someone at the market and ask him questions. So it was with Chauncey. He never belonged to Harvard, but to Cambridge. No one has caught the Socratic figure of Wright any better, I suspect, than Henry W. Holland:

. . . Having heard of Mr. Wright as an able and learned man, I went to him, and at once decided to take lessons of him in physical and mental science. It was one of the most important and fortunate events of my life. He was an extraordinary teacher for any one who really wanted to study,— always ready with explanations and illustrations of difficult points, always patient and interested. Very soon my hours with him ceased to be mere recitation, and our time was spent more in discussing the points that the lesson raised than in repeating the words of the textbook. . . .

He had little society talk; but he could converse brilliantly at a dinner table or over the later cigar. He was, however, at his best in his own study,— with his gray dressing-gown on, and with his regularly filled pipe. There many men sought him, as I did, for information or suggestion; and those who came once seldom failed to come again.[12]

There it was that C. S. Peirce, William James, Oliver Wendell Holmes, Jr., and other young bright intellectual hopefuls of Cambridge sought out the

Socrates of Bow Street and Little's Block. There it was that they came to feel the fullness of their power, drawn out by the wise talk of their older friend.

Wright traveled to Europe in 1872, although he scarcely took the Grand Tour. He could not abide art museums or fancy restaurants, and he secretly preferred the Berkshires to the Alps. He could recall an historically interesting spot only if some happy generalization had occurred to him there. The interest people showed in history seemed utterly incredible to him. Did he introduce himself to philosophers and scientists—the only people who could have interested him? Well, yes and no—his indolence caused him difficulty even here. He thought many times of arranging a meeting with Mill, but he never managed it. When he had sufficient energy he felt too shy for it. When he read Leslie Stephen's commemorative notice of Mill in the *Nation* on June 15, 1873, Wright's thoughts returned to his missed opportunity. "I think Mr. Stephen's personal recollections of him quite interesting; yet I do not know whether I really regret not seeing him last fall. I somehow never had the kind of interest in the personality of men whom I have admired for their works that many have, or at least never any strong desire to join my personality to theirs."[13] He felt that meeting a great person is like seeing his double, intimate friend, responsible agent, or even his secretary, but not *him*.

Happily Wright did visit Darwin in early September of 1872. Darwin invited him to stay overnight at Down, and the whole Darwin household contributed to what Chauncey would always remember as the social highlight of his life. He had long, fruitful talks with Darwin before the great man retired for a nap.

Wright observed, "Who would not need rest after exercising such powers of wise, suggestive, and apt observation and criticism, with judgments so painstakingly and conscientiously accurate,—unless, indeed, he should be sustained by an Olympian diet?"[14] While Darwin slept, Chauncey talked with his son Horace. He was pleased with this young host also and promised to visit him at Cambridge. "I also found Mrs. Darwin and her daughter very agreeable," he reported, "and I repent now, as I have regretted all along, that indolence has kept me so many weeks from making acquaintance with so charming a household."[15]

After his return from Europe, Wright's personal life continued fairly tranquilly, although he had isolated periods of melancholy. No doubt his irregular habits hastened his death. But he was tolerably happy the last few years of his life and worked fruitfully. The Nortons returned from Europe, and Wright made ever-increasing numbers of close friends, including Henry James, Sr., and all the members of that remarkable family. He was a frequent visitor in the James household and a favorite with them all. William James later acknowledged his indebtedness "in the old days" to Chauncey Wright and spoke almost reverently of him when Wright died. "Add to his eminence his tireless amiability, his beautiful modesty, his affectionate nature and freedom from egotism, his childlike simplicity in worldly affairs, and we have the picture of a character of which his friends feel more than ever now the elevation and the rarity."[16]

Wright died quietly while writing at his desk on Saturday evening, September 11, 1875. Henry James, the younger, was the first close friend to hear of

Wright's attack, and rushed to Mary Walker's house, though he arrived too late. James remembered Wright all through the years as one of the most doomed and tragic "bachelors of life" he had ever known. But Wright's loss was most deeply felt by Norton, Thayer and Gurney. Gurney spoke eloquently for all of them.

It is not the philosopher, but the friend, that comes so often into my memory,—more often, indeed, as time passes than when he first departed from among us. That noble head recalls not so much the massive brain as the sweet smile and the eyes that brightened with enjoyment of every touch of humor. The playfulness of his manner stands out as distinctly as the sedateness and dignity which it lighted up so charmingly. What simple dignity his manners had! . . . his manners had that stamp of innate nobility which makes, instead of learns, the rules of good-breeding. . . . He was certainly catholic in his taste among men; but, as I run over in my mind the women who found a place in his regard, I am struck with the sureness of his instinct for what is charming, refined and feminine. The friendship of such women was the strongest of testimonies, were testimony needed, to a singular rectitude and purity of soul in Chauncey, and to the native delicacy of spirit and absence of all personal claims, which make such relations cordial and easy. Like the friendship of children, which he always inspired, it gives a certain stamp as of sterling quality to the character. The praise of these would have been to Chauncey's ear the final word of commendation, and I will add no other.[17]

2. ADVOCATE OF EVOLUTION

An investigation of the manner in which Emerson, Hamilton, J. S. Mill, and Darwin successively influenced Wright's thought affords the best introduction to his philosophical development. There were other influences, to be sure, but these were the vital ones.[18]

The best judgment of Emerson, perhaps, is that he was neither a great literary artist nor a great writer of philosophy; he was rather a seer, a prophet, a great recorder of spiritual truth, a brilliant teacher and helper of those who would be self-reliant.[19] But it is difficult to get across to a modern reader of Emerson the *feel* of Emerson's greatness as a seer and moral teacher. Emerson was a man possessed, on fire morally. And it was this moral enthusiasm of Emerson's that appealed to Wright in his Harvard years. Somehow Emerson seemed more vital and alive than many of the professors. Also Emerson's criticism of historical religion appealed to young Chauncey, who, early in life and almost temperamentally it seemed, drew away from the Unitarianism of his father.

But Emerson could not long appeal to Chauncey because he never *argued* a point philosophically; he would simply state a position and hold to it on intuitive grounds. Chauncey was unhappy with this procedure because he early discovered that different people's intuitions rarely matched; so he cast about for a more tough-minded philosopher, and he found him in Sir William Hamilton, professor of philosophy at the University of Edinburgh.

Hamilton was his favorite author in the five years

immediately after his graduation from Harvard, although he had been introduced to the great philosopher earlier by Dr. Walker. In a few years all of Hamilton's work, including his book, *Philosophy of the Unconditioned* (1829), became available in this country and Wright eagerly and thoroughly studied it. After Hamilton's death, his *Lectures on Metaphysics and Logic* (1858, 1860) were also published, and Wright soon became master of these volumes as well. Indeed, in his early years, Wright's relation to Hamilton's philosophy was almost like that of a devout Christian to his Bible.

Not that he was ever given to accepting the plenary inspiration of anyone; but when he was in full sympathy with a method in philosophy, and felt a thorough respect for its representative,—as was then the case with Hamilton, and later with Mill and Darwin,—he was never weary of going back to the texts, so to speak, to find food for meditation, and starting-points for new developments and applications of his philosophical principles.[20]

Hamilton was important for Wright's development in two ways. As we have suggested, he introduced Wright to technical philosophical argumentation. Wright cut his philosophical teeth, so to speak, on Hamilton's discussion of the law of the conditioned and the nature of space. Take space as a whole, Hamilton argued,[21] it must either be limited (have a boundary) or unlimited (infinite). Since these notions are contradictory, one must be true and the other false. Yet we can neither conceive of space as limited, since any segment of space presupposes being in a yet larger space, nor as unlimited, since infinity is an "unimaginable" concept; but one or the other notion *must* be true. Thus our inability to conceive something as possible, Hamilton concludes, is no argument for its actual nonexistence.

He generalizes such conclusions as this in his famous law of the conditioned. All that can be positively thought "lies between two opposite poles of thought, which, as exclusive of each other, cannot, on the principles of identity and contradiction, both be true, but of which, on the principle of excluded middle, the one or the other must."[22] The two mutually exclusive alternatives he calls "inconditionates." He then concludes that neither inconditionate can be conceived as possible, but nevertheless one must be the case. In later years Wright turned his own critical guns on Hamilton. How, after all, Wright asked,[23] can we say we have no knowledge whatever of these inconditionates when we know that the law of excluded middle applies to them?

The wealth of scholarly detail in Hamilton's books was also important for Wright's philosophical development. (Hamilton, for example, distinguished seventeen different senses of the concept enthymeme while most philosophers were only aware of two!)[24] Hamilton's thoroughness and scholarly detail helped Wright immeasurably because he was not prone to sustained reading: he got his philosophical nutriment from a few books which immediately set him off on his own philosophical meditations and discussions. Hamilton was the ideal writer to initiate Wright into philosophy since he provided more nutriment per page than any other philosopher of his day; without this thorough knowledge of Hamilton's thought, Wright's own work would never have achieved the excellence it did.

Wright eventually abandoned all that was distinctive in Hamilton's doctrines, and he gradually came to accept much of the English empirical tradition. Wright first became acquainted with this tradition in Alexander Bain's formidable tomes on *The Senses and the Intellect* (1855) and *The Emotions and the Will* (1859). He discussed these works in detail with Joseph Winlock, his astronomer friend, and as a result became interested in the work of J. S. Mill. Although interest quickly turned to admiration, it never prevented him from making a judicious estimate of Mill's work.

In his earlier years, Wright accepted many of Mill's doctrines, although he never failed to offer ingenious new defenses of them. Like Mill, he believed that Hume's definition of "cause" as "constant conjunction" was inadequate. It is not enough to say that "cause" means that two events always occur together and never apart; their constant conjunction must be unconditional, that is, there must be no conceivable way in which the conjunction could be broken down. Night and day follow each other constantly, yet neither is the cause of the other. We are able to deny their causal relation because we can conceive of a way in which their constant conjunction would be destroyed, even though we cannot in practice achieve it. We can conceive of a cosmic screen between the sun and earth which would destroy the sequences of light and dark.

Wright also followed Mill in analyzing the concept of physical object as "a permanent possibility of sensation," although, as we shall see later, he eventually went far beyond his mentor's view to an interesting new position called neutral monism. To the end of his life, Wright assiduously defended J. S.

Mill's brand of utilitarianism as his own moral philosophy.

Wright esteemed Mill's *Essay on Liberty* and the *Subjection of Women* the least of all Mill's work, believing that they exhibited too much the emotional and enthusiastic side of Mill's character. To some extent, he shared Charles Eliot Norton's view that Mill was too much influenced on these topics by his stepdaughter, Miss Taylor.[25] Her words, they felt, had an oracular value to him; and her unconscious flattery, together with the direct flattery of prominent leaders of various women's rights movements, had an unhappy effect on his sympathetic and susceptible nature. To be sure, Wright himself was an advocate of women's suffrage and various other rights, but he always justified his position on the grounds of *human* rights and resisted any sentimental justification of *women's* rights.

In judging the importance of Mill's *Examination of Sir William Hamilton's Philosophy,* Wright reflects in an interesting way precisely the effect Mill had on his own relation to Hamilton. "That the reputation of Sir William Hamilton as a thinker was greatly diminished by this examination cannot be doubted. Nor can it be doubted that the pendulum of philosophical opinion has begun, through Mill's clear expositions and vigorous defense of the experience philosophy, to move again toward what was a century and a half ago the prevalent English philosophy."[26] Yet, Wright felt, the oscillations of the pendulum are continually diminishing through the progress of philosophical discussion. Wright had an unlimited confidence in what philosophical discussion can accomplish.

In 1859 Wright read Darwin's *Origin of Species* and became wholly converted to the idea that natural selection explains the mutation of species. The influence of Darwin's work was to become the greatest in his life. The way had been cleared for Wright's acceptance of Darwin's views by discussions in Cambridge between J. L. R. Agassiz and Asa Gray over the true meanings of "genus" and "species." Because Agassiz held the view that the characteristics of species are immutable, the Swiss-American naturalist became a strong opponent of Darwin's views. Asa Gray, great American botanist, believing in the relative nature of the species, became a sympathetic exponent of Darwinian principles. In addition to scientific contributions to the Darwinian controversy, he made important additions to the *logic* of Darwinian theory, showing, for example, that the concept of natural selection need not be understood as eliminating the theological argument from design.[27] Wright was impressed with Gray's views, and the two men talked often of botanical matters and their bearing on philosophical and logical problems. Indeed, Wright himself wrote significant scientific papers in botany, including one on phyllotaxy that was printed in the great *Lehrbuch auf Botanik.*[28]

Surprisingly enough, his early reading of *Vestiges of the Natural History of Creation* back in Northampton had also contributed to Wright's acceptance of evolutionary theory. While at Harvard he had written a paper for Dr. Walker on brute and human intellect which not only exhibited an evolutionary point of view but specifically reflected the influence of Chambers' book.[29] Gurney, however, would have us think otherwise: he wrote that Wright's "conversion" to the evolutionary viewpoint was abrupt and all a result of reading Darwin.[30] This matter of predisposition toward evolutionary theory, or lack of it, is a matter of relative emphasis. The best analysis of the case, I suspect, is this: Wright was early impressed with evolutionary notions, which he got from Chambers, but grew increasingly suspicious of the scientific credentials of those who supported them. The real scientists, like Baron Cuvier, seemed to be on the other side. Thus the real significance of Darwin, for Wright, is that he changed all this, putting the fact of evolution on a scientific basis and offering an explanation of it—the concept of natural selection—which avoided all teleological elements. This fitted into the Galilean conception of science, which was the only one acceptable to Wright.

Wright's interest in Darwinian theory, of course, was not primarily biological but also logical and philosophical. Some of his most important articles in the *North American Review*, his "definition and defense of Darwinism,"[31] are analyses of logical questions about the meaning of "explanation" in biological sciences, its relation to explanation in other sciences, and the meanings of words like "accident," "species," "class," and "transmutation." In these articles, and in his critique of Herbert Spencer's philosophy where he analyzed the nature of scientific explanation in general,[32] Wright became America's first technical philosopher of science—that is, a philosopher who analyzes the structure of scientific thought itself instead of using the results of science, as Herbert Spencer and John Fiske did, for speculative purposes.

Darwin himself was impressed with Wright's logical prowess, particularly so with his reply to St. George Mivart's *Genesis of Species* (1871). Mivart, an English biologist, had accepted the concept of evolution but had rejected, partly for theological reasons, Darwin's explanation of it in terms of natural selection. Wright felt that Mivart misrepresented and misunderstood various logical and biological points, and this feeling of misrepresentation launched him on his logical definition and defense of Darwinism. Wright sent a copy of his paper, also entitled "The Genesis of Species," to Darwin on June 21, 1871, along with a note saying, "My special purpose has been to contribute to the theory by *placing* it in its proper relations to philosophical inquiries in general."[33]

This letter began a correspondence with Darwin which lasted until Wright's death. To Wright's first letter, Darwin replied, "I have hardly ever in my life received an article which has given me so much satisfaction as the review which you have been so kind as to send me. . . . Will you provisionally give me permission to reprint your article as a pamphlet?"[34] Needless to say, Wright agreed; and the pamphlet duly appeared and was distributed in England by Darwin. Darwin's recognition of Wright prompted Mivart to reply; and Wright, who would probably have written nothing if he had not been stimulated by controversy, wrote another long article. Then there was Alfred Russel Wallace to reply to, and Wright was on his way. . . .

Chapter 2

RELIGION

1. A RELIGIOUS SKEPTIC

American Unitarianism of the nineteenth century remained close to orthodox Christianity. As the name suggests, Unitarians did not accept the Holy Trinity, but they still believed Christ to be "an intermediate divine being, a messenger supernaturally and uniquely endowed and sent as a special, indispensable revelation to man."[1] Moreover, Unitarians accepted biblical authority and insisted upon faith in Christ as necessary for salvation. As a child, Wright held this Unitarian version of Christianity but in his mature years he became an agnostic and religious skeptic. He did not renounce his religious heritage all at once or undergo any emotional rebellion; he simply drifted away from it, gradually and painlessly, as the passing years brought him new insights into his cwn life and the world around him.

Whatever we hope or believe, Wright said, it is clear that we cannot *know* that God exists. His first reason for making such a claim is this: the traditional arguments that supposedly prove the existence of God—the arguments from first cause and from design, for example—are weak and easily refuted. He never wrote systematically on the philosophy of religion, however, and we know his views only on the argument from design.[2]

Theists have claimed that evidences of design in the world prove that a benevolent God exists. A shipwrecked man is adrift in a raft and about to die of starvation when sea gulls land on his raft. He seizes and devours them and is sustained until a passing ship rescues him. Such an unlikely benefit could not have occurred by chance; it must have been designed and, hence, there must be a benevolent designer, God. Or look at the way in which species are beautifully adapted to their environment. Here is a species of butterfly that is concealed from its enemies by protective coloration—certainly such an adaptation of means to end could not have occurred by chance but must have been designed. Wright took a dim view of claims like these, arguing that they assumed the very point at issue.[3] If you already believe in God, then, of course, sea gulls-to-the-aid and leaf-colored butterflies can be taken as instances of design. But then design is unnecessary to prove that God exists. On the other hand, if the question of God's existence is genuinely open, then these instances of so-called design do not establish it.

In order to be clear about Wright's point, let us apply it to our two examples. There are, no doubt, many similar cases of men on rafts when no sea gulls appeared and the men perished. What has happened to the design in the world? The theist replies that in these other cases God has some larger good in mind —we know not what—and thus design is still present. But this reply will not do. If anything that happens in the world can be construed as a result of design, in spite of its contrast with what ordinarily counts as design, then obviously one already believes in a benevolent God. On the other hand, if the question of God's existence is really left open, then the coming of the sea gulls proves nothing, for there are innumerable counterinstances. The same outcome attends the butterfly case. Zoologists believe that they can give a scientific explanation of species adaptation, in terms of natural selection, which involves no reference to design whatever. The theist replies that the achievement of species adaptation through natural selection principles is itself part of God's plan and hence design is still at work. However, if any adaptation can be construed as a result of design, in spite of its scientific explanation, then obviously one already believes in God. On the other hand, if the question of God's existence is really left open, then adaptation of species proves nothing because it can be explained without design.

Furthermore, Wright felt that the theist's efforts to prove God's existence through design led him into devious and undesirable dealings with the growing body of scientific knowledge.[4] The theist looks to the sciences for evidences of design and development, and he rejects out of hand any scientific theory which seems to suggest the opposite. His reaction to Darwin's concept of natural selection is a good example of this behavior. According to Darwin, all possible variations in a species occur, some of which turn out to have greater adaptive value than others. The members of the species with the more useful variations are naturally selected and the others naturally eliminated. This explanation of adaptation, then, appears entirely mechanical and without design, so theists by and large instantly rejected it. Only when people like Asa Gray argued that natural selection did not necessarily destroy the argument from design (perhaps natural selection itself is a part of God's overall plan) were theists willing to accept this new scientific notion.

Wright's strongest attack against theism and design occurs in his "Natural Theology as a Positive Science" published in the *North American Review* for January, 1865.

> When a proof of special design is invalidated by the discovery that a particular effect in the operations of nature, which previously appeared to result from a special constitution and adjustment of certain forces, is really a consequent of the general properties of matter,—when, for example, the laws of planetary motion were shown to result from the law of universal gravitation, and the mathematical plan of the solar system was seen to be a consequent of a single universal principle,—the harm, if there be any, results from the theologian's mistakes, and not from the corrections of science. He should refrain from attributing any special plan or purpose to the creation, if he would find in science a constant support to religious truth. . . .[5]

Wright's second reason for saying that we cannot *know* that God exists is this: religious beliefs cannot be verified "by the particulars of concrete experience of a kind common to all. . . ."[6] The statement "This table is green" counts as knowledge because not only I see the color green when I look at the object but other people also report having the same color experience. To be sure, someone might disagree with everyone else and insist that the table is some other color. But his disagreement would cause no trouble since we could explain it by demonstrating that he is color-blind. Complicated scientific statements also count as knowledge because they can be verified (or confirmed) in a similar way. The statement "There is an electric current in this wire" counts as knowledge because not only I see the magnetic needle move, or feel the resistance coil grow hot, but other people also report having the same experiences. But religious statements or beliefs, Wright said, are quite different. Religious beliefs based on revelation and mysticism are private affairs, reflecting some individual's special experience or insight, which cannot be verified by the particulars of concrete experience which anyone can perceive.

Andrews Norton, a Unitarian theologian and father of Wright's friend Charles Norton, argued that Christian beliefs constitute knowledge because they are verified in sense experience, namely in the witnessing of miracles;[7] but Wright had no difficulty in refuting this view, since miracles never seem to be *publicly* perceived. They always seem to be witnessed by devotees.

Wright concluded that religious beliefs, whether based on revelation, mysticism or miracles, do not qualify as knowledge, although they may be accepted quite legitimately as tenets of *faith* by anyone who wishes to do so. Wright added that religious people unhappily often confuse such faith with knowledge, although Saint Paul himself warned against this deception.[8]

Wright also argued against accepting Christianity, or any other theistic religion, on faith; for any theistic religion encounters the insoluble problem of evil. According to the theist, God is all powerful and all good. Yet how can one square these characteristics with the apparently enormous amount of unnecessary evil in the world? If God is all powerful He should be able to remove such evil; and if He is all good He should want to remove it; but He does not. Why? Theists have offered various solutions to show that God's all powerfulness and all goodness are compatible with the existence of great evil. Evil builds character; evil is necessary to understand and appreciate the good of life; evil tests man's faith; evil is the result of man's misuse of free will; evil is only an illusion, producing good in the long run or from an overall viewpoint—these are the most popular of the theist's solutions. Wright, again, did not systematically discuss the problem of evil, but he does discuss the last solution, sometimes called the ultimate harmony view.[9]

The ultimate harmony solution has been historically a most influential one, and many theists consider it to be their strongest answer. The solution is usually presented in a metaphorical way, and the favorite metaphor is a musical one. A chord heard in isolation may sound dissonant and ugly but when heard in context blends into a perfect whole or an ultimate harmony. So it is with evil. What human beings call evil is an event seen out of context, in isolation, and since man has only a fragmentary view of events this is the only way he can see it. God, however, who has a "bird's-eye view" of events, sees how such events are good in the long run or good from an overall viewpoint. This viewpoint has the important consequence that evil is only an appearance, an illusion; what we ordinarily call evil is, after all, good. Consequently, whatever is, is right. Hence the ultimate harmony view is sometimes called "philosophical optimism."

J. S. Mill, Wright felt, argued effectively against

this view in the following way. Mill said, in effect:[10] In everyday life, I know what to call evil or wrong because I can plainly see its wrongness. Now if a God requires that what I ordinarily call wrong in human behavior I must call right when he does it; or that what I ordinarily call wrong I must call right because he does, even though I do not see the point of it, and if by my refusing to do so he can sentence me to Hell, to Hell I will gladly go.

H. L. Mansel, a contemporary critic of Mill, offered the following counterargument.[11] Consider the moral relations between a father and son. Certainly a father knows moral principles of action that are unknown to his son. Now would it not be presumptuous for a son to say to his father that he could not accept as right anything of which he did not plainly see the rightness. Would it not be presumptuous to say, "Father, rather than call right what you call right—which I cannot, since this is not what I mean by right—I would be willing to go to . . ."—but Mansel does not repeat Mill's alternative. He asks, however, is it not just possible that there may be as much difference between man and God as there is between a child and his father.

Wright did not find Mansel's analogy very convincing. We need, Wright said, to make the parallel more exact.[12] The child rightly has faith in his father's wisdom about things unknown to him. But the point is this: the child infers this wisdom from the wisdom and goodness of his father which he has seen and understood. He is, in short, as in all areas of thought, reasoning from the known to the unknown. With man and God, however, the case is quite otherwise. We are asked to accept God's "higher" morality, where wrong "ultimately" is right, when the only thing we know about it is that it runs counter to all that we ordinarily know about morality. We are asked, in effect, to forget the little we know of right and wrong, abdicate our intelligence, submit ourselves to something we know not of, and all this out of blind devotion to the God about whom we wish to raise serious questions. If a child followed such a course of action toward his father, we should not think it an act of deep filial piety at all but one of abject submission. If man followed such a course of action toward God, Wright felt,[13] it would be equally a case of abject submission.

2. THE IMPORTANCE OF THERAPY

Christians sometimes use "practical" arguments for believing in the existence of God and immortality—that is, arguments which try to show that happy consequences follow from believing and unhappy ones from not believing. One such argument for the existence of God and immortality is that this life itself would be meaningless and pointless if there were no God or immortality. Alfred Lord Tennyson has dramatized this view in his poem *In Memoriam*. Tennyson, along with Shakespeare, was Wright's favorite poet so we may assume he was quite familiar with the following lines:

> My own dim life should teach me this,
>> That life shall live for evermore,
>> Else earth is darkness at the core,
> And dust and ashes all that is;

This round of green, this orb of flame,
    Fantastic beauty; such as lurks
    In some wild poet, when he works
Without a conscience or an aim.

What then were God to such as I?
    'Twere hardly worth my while to choose
    Of things all mortal, or to use
A little patience ere I die;

'Twere best at once to sink to peace,
    Like birds the charming serpent draws,
    To drop head-foremost in the jaws
Of vacant darkness and to cease.

There are numerous variations on this argument, Wright said: for example, if God does not exist, moral effort is pointless; if religious questions are not answered, life cannot hold any significant value for us; and if one does not believe in God, one's life lacks any motives and drives. This sort of argument "even goes so far as to declare man's life utterly worthless, unless it is to be prolonged to infinity," and "the worth of any part—say a year's life—is infinitesimal, even if filled with the purest enjoyments, the noblest sympathies, and the most beneficent activities."[14]

Wright deflected Tennyson's argument in a straightforward way. "I have no desire to wake into a strange, unknown future life, and I can discover no valid reasons for any confidence in such a waking."[15] He simply could not himself feel that ardent desire for immortality native to some people. And he gently tried to dissuade his old Sunday-school teacher, Reverend Ellis, from believing that such a craving is any evidence that the thing craved actually exists.

I did not quite convince Dr. Ellis, I think, that his sense of indestructible vitality, even at the lowest ebb of strength, spirits, and purpose, was not good evidence that he was going to last forever, though I charged his personality with being only a set of inveterate habits. But I was interested to find that he, with other conservative thinkers with whom I have talked, regarded this evidence as good only for the individuals who feel it. This tenet may spring from an unconscious proselyting spirit,—an indirect compulsion of one by leaving one out in the cold.[16]

As this quotation shows, Wright was beautifully sensitive to the nuances of practical Christian persuasion.

While one can blunt the Christian's practical arguments in various ways, Wright was convinced that the final answer to a view like Tennyson's is not argumentative but therapeutic. If a person does not find this life significant in its own right, independent of religious questions, then he will never be convinced by arguments which purport to show it is; what he needs instead is *help* in experiencing life's intrinsic value.

The cure should not be "heroic," since this method attacks the patient as well as the disease. Opening to his activity a mental and moral and even philosophical life, infinitely varied in objects which invite attention and incite to effort, and wide enough for a rational spirit of speculation (the pursuits of positive science and their various directions),—complete preoccupation is the treatment.[17]

The therapeutic approach is useful also in the supposedly rational discussion of religious views. Sometimes a religious thinker becomes so emotionally bound up in his own views that he is incapable of appreciating the force of counterviews and counterarguments. By therapeutic measures one might successfully remove his opponent's blocks to understanding, although he might not thereby produce a change in his opponent's view. Rather he might produce an improvement of the view, for his opponent is now at least able to understand the criticism and perhaps successfully to meet it. To his friend Francis E. Abbot, liberal Unitarian minister, Chauncey applied a mild dose of mental hygiene for a slightly different malady:

. . . I was conscious of . . . attacking under indirect forms not his opinions, but the still too superstitious spirit in which he seemed to me to hold them,—in which he seemed to attribute still, in his understanding, the weight of valid evidence to the force of merely associated interests. To dissociate these interests, not to criticize his doctrines, was my only end in the debate; and I should not be willing to enter again into any such debate, except it be again with a person equally candid, unprejudiced, and intelligent,—certainly not with the public.[18]

3. IS THE SKEPTIC IRRELIGIOUS?

Needless to say, no one likes to be called "irreligious": it is one of those words which suggests so much more than it says. So it was with Wright. He not only did not want to be called irreligious but claimed, quite to the contrary, that there is a perfectly good sense in which an agnostic, skeptic, naturalist or whatever, *is* religious.[19] If his motivation in doing an act is of the proper kind, then he can be said to be acting on "principle," or religiously.

In order to make Wright's point clear, we need to compare different types of moral acts. A practical joker might wish to cry "fire" in a crowded theatre but refrains from doing so. His restraint is morally desirable, to be sure, avoiding a catastrophe, but he may well have been motivated to do the right thing only out of fear of legal sanctions, arrest and punishment. A further example: a strong swimmer jumps into a raging torrent in view of many helpless onlookers and saves a boy from drowning. This act, again, is quite desirable morally, but the swimmer may well have been motivated to do the right thing only out of fear of moral sanctions, the scornful and chilly response of his friends had he let the boy drown. On the other hand, he might have been motivated to do the right act precisely because he felt it to be his duty. Whenever a person acts in this way, from a pure love of duty, doing a right act for its own sake and not simply from fear of legal and moral sanctions, then, Wright said, he is acting on principle or *religiously*.

This is the religious idea of duty, as distinguished from those acts whose sanctions are external, either in the legal exercise of power or in the free exercise of opinion and favor. Neither force nor favor, neither negative nor positive external sanctions, are the adequate grounds of action to the truly religious soul. Whether the doctrine of a future life (rewarding by external benefits and punishing by external evils) is true or not, the true idea of religious duty is independent of it. This idea rests wholly on the value of the act *per se,* to the agent,—on the happiness it gives him, or the misery he suffers from omitting to do it.[20]

Wright was quick to point out that in this meaning of "religious," the motivations of traditional religions may or may not be religious. If one acts "because it is God's will," then, paradoxically, he is not acting religiously. He acts because it is God's will, not because it is *his duty.* Clearly, Wright said,[21] Calvinists and other extreme Protestant groups err in telescoping together all duties—legal, moral, and religious—under the prototype of the legal by making the sanction of all acts the fear of God or, conversely, the love of God.

Yet Wright was sometimes uneasy about using the word religious in his new sense. He realized that he was giving an old word new meaning, and he wanted to avoid the appearance of trying to salvage the emotional connotations of the old word. He wrote to Charles Norton in 1867, "I have yielded one point to you by using the words 'religion' and 'religious' in their unhistoric . . . sense, against my last summer's protest. I felt then a prejudice against these words, as falsely uniting the noblest feelings with the meanest ideas; as being of those *good* words through which one of the subtlest forms of tyranny is exercised over freedom of thought."[22] Wright does not tell us why he changed his mind and decided to use the term anyway, although he might simply have decided he had as much right as anyone to these positive emotional overtones. Possibly he came to believe that the word religious in his sense is the one that deserves, or ought to have, the positive emotional overtones.

Wright pointed out another sense in which agnostics and empiricists can be said to be religious. Whatever is the object of man's highest concern, he observed, might justly be called his religious object. In this case, the agnostics and empiricists have a religious object as much as anyone else, namely, society and its welfare. To people like Mill and Comte this object is the only genuinely worthy one, and Wright apparently agreed. But, he said,[23] such devotion is a matter of character, not intellect. And J. S. Mill, he felt, was the perfect example of such a devoted character.

4. A NON-THEISTIC COSMOLOGY

According to Wright,[24] the Christian views the universe essentially along dramatic lines. It is like a good play, exhibiting the dramatic unities of Aristotle: it had a beginning, is developing, and will have a denouement. The magical words of Christianity have always been "in the beginning" God created the heavens and the earth. The universe is now progressing toward its goal. The denouement is yet to come. It is called Judgment Day.

Wright never found this theistic view of the universe appealing. People are always goal directed, going some place; would it not be refreshing if the universe got nowhere? Wright believed that the universe is uncreated and eternal and that it exhibits no unfolding of a planned destiny.

... [Wright] denied creation, and held that the order of nature is not, in its cosmical relations, a progression toward an end, or a development, but is rather an endless succession of changes, simple and constant in their elements, though infinite in their combinations, which constitute an order without beginning and without termination.[25]

The production of stellar systems, Wright said, shows on the whole no development or evolution toward a goal. Systems of worlds come and go through infinite amounts of time; in the heavens there is a doing and undoing without end. This periodical shifting of events forward and backward, always changing but never getting anywhere, reminded Wright of the weather on our own planet. Hence, he called the shifting of stellar events a kind of weather itself—cosmic weather.[26]

Wright defended his eternal, repetitive, nonpurposive view of the universe in several ways. First, he claimed that if God had created the universe it would exhibit exact and regular laws.[27] The world itself would exhibit the laws that the physicist extracts from highly artificial and refined laboratory situations. Gases would follow Boyle's law exactly instead of only approximately as all known gases do. The universe, in short, if God managed it, would exhibit archetypal regularities. The concrete courses of events in the universe, however, are corrupt mixtures of lawfulness and apparent accident. All the events are caused, to be sure, but the causes become so complicated and entangled that they present the appearance of accident. They become so involved and interwoven that concrete events, as distinct from laboratory events, cannot be predicted or, in any case, cannot be predicted reliably and specifically. The world as it is, uncontrolled and wild, exhibits none of the archetypal character that one would expect if it were a product of God's orderly mind. Or would the theist rather conclude that God himself is disorderly, as wild as the world he created?

Second, Wright defended his view of the universe by what he called the principle of countermovements: a principle according to which there is no action in nature to which there is not some equivalent or commensurate counteraction.[28] He believed that such a principle was suggested by the conservation laws of physics and by the logical structure of the laws of mechanics, although he neither believed this principle to be a generalization of such facts nor strictly proved by them. Apparently Wright simply had this idea in mind: given these facts, his principle was a good working hypothesis.

Wright's principle of countermovements seems to be in difficulty immediately, however, since it ignores the second law of thermodynamics, according to which there is a tendency in the universe toward the dissipation of energy. Some philosophers have concluded that this dissipation will eventuate in the destruction of the universe—a dramatic denouement indeed! In any case, the second law does not seem to bolster Wright's notion that there is no action in nature to which there is not some equivalent or commensurate counteraction.

In his article "The Philosophy of Herbert Spencer," Wright referred to the second law and admitted that it was the most obvious objection to his principle of countermovements. He met the difficulty in the following way. The second law, while undoubtedly true, refers only to the presently known limits of the universe. But what ultimately happens to the dissipated energy? Moreover, in the case of the sun's heat, "What becomes of the sun's dynamic energy, and whence do the bodies come which support this wasting power?"[29] Consequently, he says, the second law does not suggest a dramatic denouement such as the ultimate death of nature but only propounds new questions and problems.[30]

Third, Wright believed that his eternal, repetitive, nonpurposive view can be defended indirectly, like all philosophical theories. It is notorious that philosophers generally do not try to prove their own theories directly but attempt to justify them by showing their only alternatives must be wrong. Wright felt that this strategy was perfectly legitimate, as long as it was not the only reason given for accepting a particular view. Since he believed that he had good reasons for not believing in a theistic God, he thought that he also had good reasons for rejecting the theistic view of the universe along dramatic lines. Hence, indirectly he had good reason for accepting its only alternative, namely, his own naturalistic, nonteleological world view.

Wright believed that the nebular hypothesis, in his time the most popular explanation of the origin of the solar system, ignored the principle of countermovements and exhibited instead the dramatic unities.[31] According to Laplace, the most systematic exponent of the nebular hypothesis, our sun and its planets evolved from primordial clouds of superheated gases called nebulae. The parts of the gaseous matter attracted each other, and this attraction caused the nebulae to take the shape of a globe. As the mass condensed and grew smaller, the speed of its rotation became greater. This rotary motion not only flattened the poles of the globe but also caused rings of gaseous material at the center of the globe to fly into space where they gradually collected into other globes and became satellites or planets of the sun. The same process explains the occurrence of the satellites of the planets themselves, such as the earth's moon.

Wright believed that Laplace's hypothesis exhibited the dramatic unities because the solar system, in this view, must have a beginning, a development and an end—namely, the primordial nebulae, where the word primordial, he thought, meant first created; a development through attraction, etc.; and a final culmination in the present, immutable state of the solar system.[32] Wright did not object to the nebular hypothesis, however, as mere theological speculation; far from it. He regarded it as a perfectly respectable scientific hypothesis which, if it accounted for all the facts, had to be accepted in spite of its dramatic unity. But he was convinced, certainly, that it did not explain all the astronomical facts. In fact, it went directly against some of them. Yet it persisted as the most popular explanation of the origin of the solar system in spite of its scientific deficiencies. Wright ascribed this fact to its appeal to the theistic predilections of the majority of men. It allowed a place for the magical Christian words "in the beginning" and also allowed the universe to get somewhere.

Wright worked out his own technical explanation of the origin of the solar system and of the origin of the sun's heat—an explanation, he felt, which not only successfully explained the astronomical facts but also exhibited the principle of countermovements.[33] In his explanation, he relied particularly on the law of the conservation of angular momentum and the first law of thermodynamics (the conservation of energy principle). His theory is interesting and sophisticated; although, like all nineteenth-century cosmologies, it has been outmoded by discoveries in modern physics and astronomy. The outmoding of his cosmological theory would not have surprised Wright. We must never lose sight, he said, of the inexact nature of cosmological speculation. Of the general cosmological effects, the opposing actions of heat and gravitation, the great dispersive and concentrative principles of the universe, we can at present only form vague conjectures. Nevertheless, he concluded, it seems that the most rational supposition we can form is "that these two principles are the agents of vast countermovements in the formation and destruction of systems of worlds, always operative in never-ending cycles and in infinite time. . . ."[34]

Chapter 3

MORALITY

1. MORALITY OR SKEPTICISM?

The problem of moral responsibility is a thorny one.
It arises in the following way. Modern science seems
to provide a notion of cause which implies that if
something is caused then it could not be other than
it is. If I have a genuine instance of a cause, then
a certain effect *must* occur. It could not be otherwise,
for if something else *could* occur then the cause is
still unknown. If the concept of cause applied only
to physical objects there would be no problem, but
it also applies to human behavior and here the problem begins. If a person's behavior is caused, then
he must act in a certain way. He could not have
acted any differently than in fact he did act. On the
other hand, moral judgments are meaningful only
if it *is* possible to say that a man could have acted
differently than he did. If I say, "You should not
have stolen that money," I am assuming that you
could have acted in two different ways: you could
have either stolen the money or refrained from doing so, and that is why I am able to hold you responsible for what you did and to condemn you for
making the wrong choice.

At this point, causality and moral responsibility
come into direct conflict.[1] If human behavior is
caused, it could not be different from what it is; but

if human behavior is morally responsible, then it could have been different. The conclusion is unavoidable that human behavior cannot both be caused and morally responsible—it has to be one or the other. If one believes that behavior is caused and thus not morally responsible, he is a determinist and moral skeptic. He believes that moral judgments are meaningless noises. If one believes that behavior is morally responsible and thus not caused, he is an indeterminist and believes that moral judgments are meaningful and defensible. Wright wished to avoid the skepticism of traditional determinism, but he was firmly convinced that indeterminism was not the way to do it.

Wright, however, did full justice to the indeterminist position. A person defending this position, he said,[2] does not hold the odd notion that no human behavior is caused. He would happily agree that psychology, economics, and other sciences of man tell us a great deal about the causes of learning, perception, market fluctuations, and so on; but he would insist, nevertheless, that in choice situations there is finally an undetermined decision for which the agent is responsible. However, there is a difficulty immediately obvious even on this view. If the indeterminist strictly means that choices are not caused at all, then he must admit that the agent who acted one way under certain conditions may later act in a completely different way under the same conditions, even though the agent has not changed at all. Instead of introducing moral responsibility, the indeterminist simply introduces caprice. Moral responsibility demands the presence of something positive rather than merely the absence of causality.

Moreover, Wright criticized the indeterminist be-

cause there is no positive evidence for his position.[3]
When the indeterminist says, "Look, here is an example of undetermined choice," one has no trouble
at all in replying, "It is true that we do not *know*
the cause of this event but surely this ignorance does
not imply that the event is in reality causeless."
Wright pointed out that we often do not know what
the state of the weather will be tomorrow, but this
incapacity reflects complexity of causes, not their
absence. So it is with human behavior. Moreover,
Wright added,[4] the notion that everything has a cause
is a postulate or presupposition of all scientific and
common-sense thinking. It would make no sense to
look for the causes of behavior, physical or human,
if one thought they did not exist.

Finally, to the indeterminist's claim that man
directly experiences freedom in choice situations,
that he is introspectively aware of it and needs no
argument to convince him of it, Wright replied as
follows. No one wants to deny psychological facts,
and it is a fact that men invariably feel that they
choose freely. It is wrong to think, however, that
this feeling is a sign of the absence of any cause of
our choice. The feeling of freedom amounts simply
to this: If a man puts a gun at my head and demands
my wallet, I "decide" to give it to him. But I have
no feeling of freedom because I was coerced or compelled to do it. On the other hand, if I consider carefully the consequences of giving all the money in my
wallet to a derelict, and decide to do so, I have a
feeling of freedom because I was not compelled to
do it. The feeling of freedom in choice situations,
then, indicates the absence of coercion, not the absence of causality.[5]

Wright suggested a far better way of meeting the

determinist's moral skepticism. Clearly, he said, the behavior of human beings can be caused in two quite different ways. Heredity and early environment are external causes over which we have no control but which, nevertheless, in part at least, have made us the way we are. To the extent that these external factors control behavior a person is not free and morally responsible. On the other hand, reason, imagination and a host of other subtle motives are internal causes over which we have control and which also, to some extent, have made us the way we are. To the extent that *these* factors control behavior, a person is morally responsible. This notion of a reasonable human being who is able to consider the consequences of his acts, rather than that of un-caused choice, is what people in ordinary life mean by being morally responsible. Therefore, according to Wright, although all behavior is caused, some behavior is still morally responsible, namely that which is internally, or self, caused.[6] Wright touched on these views succinctly in a letter to Simon New-comb on May 18, 1865.

. . . The world has been deceived for more than sixteen centuries by metaphors invented by some Alexandrian Platonists speculating on the nature of virtue. Sects, schisms, and strifes have been the consequents of these unfortunate metaphors drawn from Roman law. While everybody recognizes as real those feelings which we describe as a sense of moral freedom and the feeling of responsibility, few attend to the metaphorical character of the names which are given to them. "The virtuous man is free," said the Platonic philosopher. "He is, like a Roman citizen, uncontrolled by a master." "A

vicious man is a slave." Such is the metaphor: now
what is the real character so described? This freedom is internal control in place of external control;
centric or self control, which, so far from making
a man free, in the scientific sense of the word
[that is, uncaused], makes his life regular and his
conduct calculable. He has a freedom like that of
the solar system or like that of a normal growth.
Again, moral responsibility was so named from
legal responsibility in Roman law; and the sense of
it is only the sense of dignity and trustworthiness
which is characteristic of moral feeling, a sense
of being intrusted with interests not his own. . . ."[7]

Wright's concept of internal or self cause, important as it is, is not a completely adequate reply to
the traditional determinist. Let us imagine how a
determinist might counter it. He would say that rational behavior itself has causes and hence *it* must
be what it is. When we reason, we think we can decide either one way or another; but in reality, since
this reasoning itself is caused, the outcome of our
deliberation could not have been different from what
it was. Wright never considered this reply of the determinist, although it is interesting to see that he has
a possible answer to it implicit in his views on causality. A cause, Wright said,[8] may give rise to an effect
which has distinctly new characteristics, ones which
could not have been predicted no matter how much
one knew of the nature of the cause. These novel
elements later philosophers called emergents. Wright
might have applied this concept to the determinist's
claim in the following way: It is true that reasoning
ability, like everything else in the world, is caused;
but once caused it brings into play genuinely new

capacities. Reasoning is emergent in respect to its causes; having been brought into existence, it allows one to consider alternative acts unmolested by the "must" aspect of lower causes. Reasoning, in short, once caused, is itself a new kind of cause.

2. THE GREATEST HAPPINESS PRINCIPLE

By presenting a feasible alternative to traditional determinism, Wright successfully avoided moral skepticism; he was then free to construct his own moral system. He became a utilitarian, which means that he believed one ought always to strive to produce the greatest amount of happiness for the greatest number of people.[9] This principle, however, is not as simple as it sounds. Consider the following concrete case:

A doctor promises to tell his patient the exact state of his health after an examination. But the doctor discovers that the patient is seriously ill and needs a major operation. He also believes that the patient's knowledge of the seriousness of the operation will almost certainly interfere with its success. As a utilitarian, then, apparently the doctor must lie to his patient, for only in this way can he produce the happiest consequence for him. But the situation is not that simple for a utilitarian. He must take into account also the effects of lying, both on himself and on his patients should they learn he lied. How will it affect his own character and how will it affect the confidence of patients? He must also consider whether the patient involved might act in a way detrimental to his health out of ignorance of the seriousness of his illness. The likelihood of *all* these consequences involved in the case must be carefully examined before the utilitarian can decide what act will produce the greatest amount of happiness for the greatest number of people.

Wright defended this utilitarian view against numerous criticisms. In fact, he devoted most of his writing in moral philosophy to this job. The criticisms and how Wright met them follow.

(a) The trouble with the principle of utility is that it neglects the *intentions* of the moral agent.[10] After all, a scoundrel can accidentally do an act which has good consequences and a kind person one which has evil consequences, but the former act is not therefore right nor the latter one wrong. Wright demurred. Certainly if a scoundrel saves someone from drowning, whatever his motives, the consequences of the act are good and hence the *act is* right. Wright admitted that it is important for people to act with good intentions, but this fact, he felt, could be accounted for perfectly well within a utilitarian framework. Even though acting from good intentions sometimes produces disastrous consequences, nevertheless, according to utilitarians, acting from good intentions is desirable because in the long run more desirable consequences will be produced thereby. In Wright's words,

. . . what is called the conscience, or strong and compelling aversions to certain classes of actions and admirations or approvals of other classes, should be respected and carefully fostered, even though in some matters it leads wrong; since a faulty conscience is more useful or less harmful on the whole than unprincipled conduct. . . .[11]

(b) Another difficulty with the utilitarian view is that it depends upon judging what are the likely consequences of alternative acts.[12] It is a notorious fact that we are often ignorant of what the future holds and that our expectations and predictions fail dismally. We see a friend walking by our house in the rain and call to him to seek shelter. As he turns into our walk he is struck by lightning and killed instantly. We tried to produce good consequences for him but, due to the unpredictability of the future, produced disastrous ones instead. Hence, we can easily see that any moral philosophy which depends upon judging the likelihood of future consequences is doomed to failure.

Wright admitted that we cannot have certain knowledge of the future: in any empirical judgment we run the risk of being mistaken. Nevertheless, he considered this less-than-certain knowledge of the future a far more objective way of reaching moral decisions than the deliverances of a person's conscience or "moral sense." Too many people, he felt, have diseased consciences; witch-hunting, in one guise or another, occurs in every century. Utility, he wrote to Norton, is vitally important as a standard for correcting a whole world of abuses "which subsist by the very same sanctions or the same kind of sanctions the intuitive morality adopts as the basis of right and wrong."[13] Prejudices sanctioned by time, evils sanctioned by habit, and religious absurdities nurtured by tradition are all abuses that "can claim the same grounds of justification as those on which the intuitive morality would base the ten commandments; namely, that most people, or at least somebody, *feel* them to be right."[14] Moreover, an earnest

conscience is not necessarily a healthy one. Earnest-
ness proves conscientiousness, not rightness.[15] The
men who lighted the fagots after a witch trial were
very earnest men indeed.

(c) Another criticism of the greatest happiness
principle is that a person confronted with the need
for making a moral decision quickly does not have
time to calculate the likely consequences of alternative acts. If he took the time, the opportunity to
act would be lost. J. S. Mill had replied that this
criticism of utilitarianism would be similar to saying
that a Christian could not act according to his principles because he would have insufficient time to con-
sult the Bible. Just as the Christian knows his principles well enough to apply them quickly to standard
cases, so the utilitarian knows the likely outcomes
of many sorts of situations well enough to apply them
quickly to standard cases.

Wright met this criticism in a more elaborate way
than Mill. While utility is always the test of right conduct, he said,[16] it cannot, and indeed should not, be
consulted every time before we act. Many actions
are performed more successfully when done instinc-
tively or habitually and are actually disrupted when
we consciously attend to their operation. The utilitarian, Wright argued, relies on these forces of instinct
and habit not for rational guidance, of course, but
for practical efficacy; "yet these are so important to
its aims, that they are not safely to be disregarded,
or unnecessarily opposed, or weakened by substitu-
ting for them habitually the calculations of ex-
pediency."[17]

Wright returned to this point on numerous occasions. To Grace Norton he wrote:

Utilitarianism needs to be supplemented, in order to meet misunderstandings, by a Philosophy of Habit, and to lay down among its practical principles that, since motives are effective, not in proportion to their usefulness or reasonableness, but rather to their singleness or instinctiveness, therefore it is reasonable to foster and to rely practically on the force of proper habits and just, natural inclinations.[18]

The relation between instinct and utility was very important for Wright because he felt that there was a close connection between Darwin's concept of natural selection and the principle of utility.[19] Indeed, Wright sometimes thought of natural selection as if it were nature's own principle of utility. He sometimes referred to natural selection as the theoretic or descriptive version of the principle of utility, although it is extremely difficult to see how any moral principle could have a factual counterpart in anything but a metaphorical sense. Charles S. Peirce, one of Wright's younger philosophical friends, criticized him for this unhappy attempt to join, in not too clear a fashion, two entirely different notions.[20]

(d) Another criticism of utilitarianism claims that it makes no provision for unselfish acts or noble self-sacrifice. Wright is genuinely surprised at this criticism because it shows such negligible understanding. Actually, he pointed out,[21] whenever a person is motivated by the principle of utility, he must consider the overall good consequences, not simply the good consequences for himself, and hence acts unselfishly. Whenever a person is motivated by this principle he is acting on principle and, in one sense of the word, is acting religiously. Moreover, Wright said, the utilitarian also practices self-sacrifice, but he wants to be sure that it counts for something by helping someone. Self-sacrifice, in short, must not be blind to what it can achieve; if it is to be a significant self-sacrifice, it must be a realistic one and take into account likely consequences.

(e) Another criticism of utilitarianism argues that it requires one to act unjustly sometimes in order to produce the greatest amount of happiness. Consider the following example. William borrows a book from Josiah and promises to return it in a month. Josiah, however, forgets that he loaned the book. William knows that he will make good use of the book but Josiah will scarcely look at it again. Consequently, he decides on utilitarian grounds to add the book quietly to his own library. To this sort of example, Wright had a ready and traditional reply. William should not have broken his promise to return the book because it might become known and have adverse effects on promise-keeping in the future. William's son might say, "I will break my promise to redeem this note, for, after all, father does not always keep his word either."

It is not difficult, however, to construct another example to which Wright's reply is irrelevant.[22] Two arctic explorers have only enough food to keep one of them alive until camp can be reached. One offers to give his food to the other, and himself perish, if the other will see that his son is given a good college education. The second one accepts the food and gives his word. Years later it turns out that the first explorer's son is a dunce while the second one's son is a genius. Moreover, the surviving explorer cannot send them both to college. On utilitarian grounds, it is clear he should break his promise to the dead explorer and send his own son to college—which, again, seems entirely unjust. And Wright's reply is irrelevant here because the breaking of the promise cannot become known and have adverse effects on promise-keeping in the future. The first explorer is dead and the second one will never tell.

(f) The most frequent criticism of nineteenth-century utilitarianism centered around the notion of happiness. After all, there are vastly different kinds of pleasures, some "low" and some "high." Sensuous pleasures are low-order, while intellectual, spiritual and aesthetic pleasures are high-order. Only the latter genuinely constitute happiness. Several questions now arise: Can the utilitarian distinguish, within his own system, between higher- and lower-order pleasures? And does the utilitarian strive for the greatest amount of sensuous pleasures for the greatest number of people—a kind of gigantic bacchanalia—or for the greatest amount of spiritual happiness for the greatest number?

To the first question, Wright answered that the utilitarian can distinguish higher- and lower-order pleasures in two ways.[23] Reading Shakespeare, say, can be distinguished as a higher-order pleasure from lower-order pleasures like drinking beer, because the pleasure in the former case lasts longer, is unmixed with unpleasant consequences and can occur more frequently. However, pleasure, whether received from reading Shakespeare or drinking beer, is intrinsically the same wherever experienced. This answer, Wright pointed out, is Jeremy Bentham's. J. S. Mill disagreed with Bentham, insisting that there were intrinsic differences among pleasures. The pleasure one experiences when reading Shakespeare is simply different from the pleasure one has in drinking beer.

Wright, like Mill, believed that there were intrinsic differences among pleasures. He emphasized this point in the following way:

> It is a mistake . . . which all, or almost all, the opponents of the utilitarian philosophy make, as well as many of its advocates, to suppose that the measure of a pleasure in this philosophy is simply its intensity as a feeling, and not also its rank or preferability in kind, or a certain dignity it has in the spiritual hierarchy independent of and antecedent to its proper moral rank.[24]

Aesthetic pleasures, particularly, he thought, have an intrinsic dignity, a preferability in kind, which marks them off from other pleasures.[25] Wright, then, was committed to saying, "Pleasure x is better than pleasure y," a judgment, moreover, which is not a calculated or reasoned conclusion of any argument but simply a matter of feeling. But does not this statement sound more like an intuitionist's than a utilitarian's? After all, the word better makes it a moral judgment and yet the judgment is defended simply on the ground of *feeling*. Wright saw quickly that he might be accused of an implicit, or at least incipient, intuitionism, but he denied his guilt steadfastly.[26] The intrinsic preferability which we experience some pleasures to possess, he warned, must not be confused with moral rank which is calculated from a consideration of general good consequences. Since experienced preferences are not yet moral concerns, the statement "Pleasure x is better than pleasure y" is not a moral one. Hence the charge of creeping intuitionism collapses.

To the second question Wright answered that he

saw nothing in the least wrong with enjoying sensuous pleasures as long as they do not interfere with the realization of higher-order pleasures also. The utilitarian does not recommend a gigantic bacchanalia, to be sure, but strives for the maximum amount of mutually compatible sensuous and spiritual pleasures. Anyway, there is something a bit odd about making the two types of pleasures always competitive, as if one could not drink a glass of beer while reading Shakespeare and enjoy both.

(g) If all other criticisms fail, the philosopher has one recourse open to him: absorb the opposing view into one's own system. Francis Wayland, pre-Civil War President of Brown University and noted moral philosopher, used this tactic against utilitarianism.

No one would doubt, Wayland wrote,[27] that the Creator intends for us to do the things which have pleasant consequences and to avoid the things which have unpleasant ones, both in our own lives and in those of others. Thus we know it is God's will for man to avoid drunkenness, for the unhappy consequences are open to the most casual inspection. The same is true for revenge, for the unhappy consequences of revenge were never more clearly seen than in the near extinction of the Indian tribes which practiced it as a duty. It is clear that Wayland was embracing a utilitarian standard, yet he enfolded it within his own theological ethics. And he was perfectly clear and explicit about this maneuver, for he wrote:

The feeling of moral obligation does not arise from the *simple fact that such a course of conduct will or will not produce the greatest amount of happiness, but from the fact that this tendency shows us what is the will of our Creator;* and we are, by the principles of our nature, under the highest possible obligations to obey that will.[28]

Wright, of course, would reject such an effort to kidnap utilitarian principles simply because it was based on natural theology (the science of deducing the existence and nature of God from experience). In the previous chapter we have seen his antipathy to any natural theology. Wright claimed that the arguments from design invariably assume the question at issue. The same holds true here for inferences about God's intentions from observed events. To be sure, unpleasant consequences attend the drunkard's behavior, but perhaps God enjoys tormenting sinners. If one is shocked by this notion, it is only because he already believes what he thinks the facts reveal, namely, God's benevolent intentions. It would seem better to keep utilitarianism in its pure form than bring it under the wing of natural theology.

3. PRACTICAL PROBLEMS

Wright's views on organized reform add much to our understanding of his practical moral concerns. His position was intermediate between the two diametrically opposed views of organized reform which were popular in the middle of the nineteenth century.

While there are many nuances in their respective views, Emerson and Thoreau represent a negative attitude toward reform movements, while George W. Curtis, Wright's friend, and Theodore Parker represent the pro-reform viewpoint.[29] The former felt that their doctrines of self-reliance and the perfectability of the soul committed them to a negative position on organized reform. Political agitation and social manipulation could attain nothing significant; the only effective reform was regeneration of the individual heart and soul. Moreover, one ought not to interfere with God's work, trying to bring about or hasten the appearance of something which may not be in his plan at all. A youthful follower of Emerson wrote that "reform becomes at last a practical atheism and, so far as organized, loses souls. . . ." Moreover, he continued:

> Reform is organized distrust. It says to the universe fresh from God's hands, "You are a miserable business; lo! I will make you fairer!" and so deputes some Fourier and Robert Owen to improve the bungling work of the Creator.[80]

Curtis and Parker, on the other hand, realized that it is little comfort for a slave to know that he will be set free when his master's heart is regenerated. And even though God is directing things, might not the efforts of man be instruments of his action? Seen in this light, organized reform movements no longer appeared to be practical atheism. Both Curtis and Parker felt that their society stifled the realization of man's self-reliance and blocked the perfectability of man's soul. It is necessary to create a social and intellectual climate in which self-realization would become possible.[81] And Curtis' and Parker's efforts in reform movements—in the abolition of slavery, the gaining of women's rights, civil service reform, and prison reform—made some notable progress toward this goal.

On organized reform, designed for utilitarian ends,

Wright had divided feelings. He could not agree with
Emerson and Thoreau certainly, for one could wait
until doomsday for the regeneration of men's hearts.
On the other hand, he had no great enthusiasm for
tinkering with society.[32] Utilitarian reason, he felt, is
but a crude guide for life; and even well-thought-out
systems of law contain little positive wisdom. Indeed, Wright said, how can we expect to legislate
into existence the conditions for happiness when
everyone has a different notion of what happiness is.
Since people will never be satisfied by the same conditions, no matter how beneficent they appear to be,
it is useless to plan for the general happiness by legal
and social reform. Thus, Wright opposed planned
marriages for utilitarian ends.[33] The sad consequences
of marriages arranged by accident or because of
momentary passion cannot be eliminated by religious,
legal, and social restrictions. Of course, certain ob-
stacles should be and are placed in the way of hasty
marriages, but positive planning to bring together
appropriate mates, he felt, was doomed to failure.

. . . As to any ill effect upon posterity of the present freedom of marriage unions, no law-givers, no
private counsellors, are at all equal to the subtle
skill of nature, shown in the survival of the fittest;
which, though a rough remedy for evils that wisdom, if it existed, might forestall, is one which
wisdom has not yet equalled. The ancient state of
Sparta, whose law givers undertook to do the work
of nature in selection, perished in consequence;
and nature selected those ancient communities
whose principles of freedom and humanity to the
weak seemed opposed to her Draconic laws. *Not
to help* natural selection is the human way, strong

in its weakness, of gaining the favor of this fatal
power; and not to legislate is often the wisest principle of legislation.[34]

Wright, however, was convinced that utilitarian
reason could do much through legislative and social
reform to *alleviate* the great suffering and injustice
everywhere manifest in the world. While one cannot
bring about happiness, one can try, with reasonable
assurance of success, to reform the social and eco-
nomic conditions which lead to misery, despair and
injustice. He felt, for example, that American women
were unjustly deprived of the vote and of equality
under the law, conditions that could be rectified by
legislation.[35] Here was an evil which, for utilitarian
reasons, surely should be eradicated without further
delay. In this matter his motivation was a utilitarian
attachment to liberty in *principle* rather than a sentimental defense of women's rights.

. . . believing, as I do, that human beings generally, even children, have hitherto been much more
in subjection to authority than they ought to be
(both directly and indirectly, or through the sanctions of punishments and rewards); . . . and seeing
that, so far as women are treated differently from
men, it is mainly in consequence of some traditional and prevailing sentiments which are not justified
by any more obvious utility than an unreasoning
conservatism,—I am in general ready to protest
against this present state of things and in favor of
larger liberty. . . . [However] it is under the rights
of individuals . . . that I would place the rights
of women; and it seems to me that those who
agitate specially for the latter are not usually

actuated by the true principle of liberty, since what they demand is not equal exemption of all persons from oppression . . . but . . . an increase of the range of authority by conferring it equally on all.[36]

In any case, Wright offered this admonition to all social planners, whether positive or negative, whose first question is "What do I do about it?"[37] They should ponder carefully, he said, these Delphic answers: "Keep knowledge at nurse as long as possible; cherish its grounds, reasons, and questions; draw conclusions only when the necessity of decision compels." "Let not your love of your neighbor mistake itself for a knowledge of him." "Don't mistake an aesthetic preference for a moral judgment or let generous feeling corrupt either justice or good taste."

Wright's views on practical morality help one to evaluate J. B. Thayer's criticism of Chauncey as morally lazy.[38] In the *Letters*, Thayer observed that his friend had permitted the scientific habit of mind to creep, unobserved, into the region of conduct. He seemed to suspend judgment on moral matters, always waiting for further evidence, until the chance for action was past. He never seemed to have any moral enterprises or to get involved in any reform movement and, indeed, seemed even to decline the unremovable burden of ordering his own life. In the light of Wright's views on reform, however, we can see clearly why he was in one way legitimately content not to undertake moral enterprises. The more we try to order our own and others' lives positively, the more likely we are to create unexpected unhappy consequences. Moral meddling, in short, is usually a dangerous thing. To be sure, Thayer's criticism is valid if Wright did nothing to alleviate suffering and

misery—a legitimate utilitarian goal on his own view.
Political or social efforts to attain this goal, of course,
were closed to him, for he lacked utterly any ability
for this sort of activity. But where personal effort
to relieve suffering was required in small and unob-
trusive ways, Chauncey was certain to be close at
hand. To the crippled and exhausted Susan Lesley,
Chauncey's care of her daughter Mary was a god-
send. To the frail Mrs. Lyman in her gloomy depression he was the only anchor to reality: he took Gurney to tea with her daily so she would have the
atmosphere she loved so dearly. To Mary Walker,
runaway slave, he was steadfast friend in all daily
matters, large or small, and trusted ally in the crucial
mission of passing on information to slaves in the
underground railroad. None of these friends would
have found in Chauncey one who was content to
have no moral enterprises at all. And Thayer's notion that his dear friend declined the unremovable
burden of ordering his life is too extreme, even naïve.
Chauncey did not decline to order his own life; he
was hopelessly and tragically unable to do so. But
that he gave a beautiful order to many other lives,
there can be no doubt.

Chapter 4

SCIENCE

Chauncey Wright was an accomplished philosopher of science. He wrote more perceptively about the structure of scientific thought than any earlier American thinker. At first he was most concerned with the logical features of science in general; although later, under Darwin's influence, he wrote increasingly about the logical aspects of evolutionary theory.

1. MISCONCEPTIONS

In his earlier discussions Wright corrected misconceptions about the logical features of science.[1] Herbert Spencer, he felt, had done more to promote these misconceptions than anyone else.

(a) Some philosophers of science seem to think that scientific hypotheses and theories are like natural history generalization. They write as if a law in physics were like the generalization "All swans are white." We see that this swan, that swan, and so on, are all white, so we generalize our evidence into the hypothesis that all swans are white. Such hypotheses are straightforward *summaries* of observation; they are what logicians call inductions by simple enumeration.

Wright abhorred above all others this notion that scientific hypotheses are simply summaries or enumerations;[2] he emphasized how little justice it did to any science which followed the pattern set by Galileo. In the first place, any scientific theory must be capable of yielding consequences about events other than those it is based on—just as the law of gravity led to the discovery of the planet Uranus. Scientific theories are not simply summaries of truth; they are also discoverers of truth. In Wright's words:

> Nothing justifies the development of abstract principles in science but their utility in enlarging our concrete knowledge of nature. The ideas on which mathematical Mechanics and the Calculus are founded . . . and the theories of Chemistry are such working ideas,—finders, not merely summaries of truth.[3]

Wright felt that Herbert Spencer had not appreciated this aspect of science or he would never have formulated his so-called law of evolution. According to Spencer's law, all natural events evolve "from homogeneity to heterogeneity through differentiation and integration." This law, Wright felt, was barbaric science as well as barbaric language! What, after all, does it accomplish? It simply summarizes the most general features common to the evolution of the solar system from nebulae to planets, the evolution of species from protozoa to man, and the evolution of society from tribes to nations: they start in a simple way and develop into more complicated forms. This law is pointless, of course, because it does not lead to any new information or observations.

However skillfully the philosopher may apply his analytical processes to the abstraction of the truths

involved in patent facts, the utility of his results
will depend not so much on their value and extent
as mere abstractions, as on their capacity to en-
large our experience by bringing to notice residual
phenomena, and making us observe what we have
entirely overlooked, or search out what has eluded
our observation. Such is the character of the principles of modern natural philosophy, both mathematical and physical. . . . But this is not the value
which we find in Mr. Spencer's speculations.[4]

In the second place, scientific hypotheses are not
natural history generalizations because they contain
abstract or theoretical concepts. Wright emphasized
that concepts like uniform motion, momentum and
acceleration do not refer to anything which can be
experienced directly; they are abstractions, related
only indirectly to experience.[5] To discover if an
object is in uniform motion, for example, one cannot
simply look at its movement but he has to calculate
whether it goes through equal distances per unit of
time. The concepts in natural history generalizations
are quite different: they all refer to things like swans
and white which are directly experienced. Thus,
natural history generalizations are summaries of observations. But scientific hypotheses cannot be summaries of observations because their concepts do not
refer to anything which can be observed.

Wright felt that Spencer never understood the
nature and importance of theoretical concepts. Whenever he used them, he always changed them in a way
that ruined their significance. Spencer used physical
concepts like force and momentum for his own
philosophical purposes—translating "conservation of
force," for example, into "persistence of force." This

latter principle, Wright said, is completely vague and indefinite, has no predictive value whatever and thus ceases to have any relation to the original scientific principle.

> Terms which the real physicist knows how to use as the terms of mathematical formulas . . . are appropriated by Mr. Spencer to the further elaboration of his vague definitions, and to the abstract description of as much in real nature as they may happen to apply to. . . . Out of mathematical formulas these terms lose their definiteness and their utility.[6]

(b) Empirical philosophers like David Hume and J. S. Mill claimed that all knowledge arises through sensory experience. When applied to science this empirical view usually held that scientific hypotheses also must be suggested by, or originate in, sensory experience. Although Wright was a member of this empirical tradition, he rejected this view.[7] The origins of a scientific hypothesis, he said, are irrelevant; an hypothesis may come from experience, imagination, intuition, dreams or any other conceivable source. The important point is that a scientific hypothesis must yield predictions which can be *verified* in sensory experience. If the predictions come true, the hypothesis is confirmed; if they fail, it is rejected.

> . . . whatever be the origin of the theories of science, whether from a systematic examination of empirical facts by conscious induction, or from the natural biases of the mind, the so-called intuitions of reason—whatever the origin, real or ideal, the *value* of these theories can only be tested . . . by

an appeal to sensible experience, by deductions from them of consequences which we can confirm by the undoubted testimony of the senses. Thus, while ideal or transcendental elements are admitted into scientific researches, though in themselves insusceptible of simple verification, they must still show credentials from the senses, either by affording from themselves consequences capable of sensuous verification or by yielding such consequences in conjunction with ideas which by themselves are verifiable.[8]

Wright's last sentence in the above quotation has an important implication for present-day philosophy of science. By ideal or transcendental elements Wright meant theoretical concepts like force, mass and atom. Such concepts, while not themselves referring to anything which can be experienced, must yield consequences which can be experienced. But not all theoretical concepts need have even this relatively close connection to experience. Some concepts may not yield any such consequences except in conjunction with other theoretical concepts. Thus, these concepts are related to experience only in a very indirect and tenuous way. It is interesting to note that present-day positivists like Rudolf Carnap have only recently come to hold this same view, after an earlier insistence that every theoretical concept must have experiential consequences.

(c) The role of experiment in science can be interpreted in two different ways—either as a way of discovering causes or as a way of verifying them. If someone suffers from a rash, which occurs soon after he eats, he might discover the cause of it by noting which food is the only one always present before the rash occurs. Francis Bacon called such a procedure the experimental method of agreement and interpreted the experimental methods in general as ways of discovering causes.[9] On the other hand, Pascal, believing that air has weight and thus exerts pressure, deduced that the pressure should decrease higher up in the blanket of air and increase lower down. He checked his deductions in the following way: when a barometer was carried up a mountain, it was noted that the mercury column in the tube was about three inches lower at the top of the mountain than at its base. This experiment *verified* the hypothesis about atmospheric pressure but certainly had nothing to do with its discovery. Physical scientists think of experiment as a way of verifying hypotheses rather than a means of discovery.

Wright, with his great knowledge of physics, emphasized, as one might expect, this verification function. He criticized Francis Bacon for interpreting the experimental methods as simply means of discovery.[10] Bacon acted as if a simple-minded use of experimental methods would mechanically lead to the discovery of laws and causes. What need is there for hypotheses? Indeed, Bacon never really understood the nature of hypotheses—systems of theoretical concepts which can be deductively elaborated—and that is the reason he missed the importance of experiment as a method of verification. Wright was quite willing to admit that experiment *may* lead to the discovery of causes. In everyday situations like that of the rash and in sciences which do not have a sophisticated system of theoretical concepts which can be deductively elaborated and tested, experiment may have some use as an instrument of discovery. But in a theoretical science like mechanics, the only real use of experiment is for verification, not discovery.

(d) Philosophers of science often claim that modern science, beginning with Galileo, developed rapidly because it utilized methods and techniques not found in ancient science. Wright, however, believed that Galilean science exhibited no radical new features not already to be found in isolated instances of Greek science.[11] The use of hypotheses, their deductive development, often through the use of mathematics, and the testing of them through experimentation—all of these crucial elements in scientific inference can be found in varying degrees of sophistication, for example, in Archimedes' work on hydraulics and Ptolemy's astronomical theory. The reason that modern science, unlike ancient, developed rapidly is that it was freed from the domination of philosophical interests, and the key to this freedom was the presentation of modern science as objective or *metaphysically neutral*.[12] Wright illustrates what he means by the metaphysical neutrality of science in the following way. The realist in metaphysics believes that physical objects exist whether or not anyone perceives them and that they are the (partial) *causes* of perception whenever it occurs. The idealist believes that physical objects exist only when perceived, for he interprets them simply as clusters of perceptions. Wright observed that the scientist is able to ignore such a question as the ultimate nature of physical objects. The astronomer, for example, finds that the planets follow certain laws; but they will follow these same laws whether planets be interpreted as physical objects or as clusters of perception. Hence, the astronomer's work is independent of such philosophical questions; it is, as Wright said, metaphys-ically neutral.

Wright thought that Bacon's real significance in the history of thought consisted precisely in his rec-ognition of this metaphysical neutrality of science. Bacon may not have understood the inner workings of the new science too well, but he had the genius to present it to the world as metaphysically neutral and thus helped to produce its rapid advancement.

> . . . indeed he [Bacon] had no system; but by mar-shaling the forces of criticism known to his time, and reinforced by his own keen invention, against all systems, past and prospective, he aimed at establishing for science a position of neutrality, and at the same time of independent respectability, between the two hostile schools of the Dogmatists and the Empiricists. . . . He thus secured the true status for the advancement of experimental sci-ence, or of experimental philosophy, as it came to be called.[13]

(e) Wright emphasized that uniform motion, mo-mentum and all the other concepts of Galilean sci-ence are free from the goal-directed, purposive or teleological quality of Aristotelian science. Aristo-telian science was value-centered in its very structure; its scientific concepts themselves were goal-directed or purposive in nature. Why should a ball in motion on a plane come to rest? Aristotle answered this question by saying that all things have a natural state of existence and that they seek to return to it when they have been deprived of it. The natural state of a heavy object like a ball is rest, and whenever a violent motion is imparted to it from outside, it seeks to return to its natural state. Galileo answered the same question differently, using no purposive concepts like "natural state" or "seeking to return." It is the generation of friction, Galileo said, which eventually stops the ball. On a frictionless plane the ball would roll forever.

Yet teleology, Wright wrote,[14] is a subtle poison. Varieties and nuances of it appear even within the Galilean framework if we are not constantly alert to the danger. The teleology he had in mind was the grafting of dramatic unities onto otherwise Galilean-type explanations. His most picturesque renunciation of this sort of teleology occurred in his discussion of biological evolution. We do not need to read any dramatic unities into the origin of species—a protozoic beginning, an increase in complexity, and a culmination in man's appearance and in the evolution of *his* societies. For all we know, Wright said,[15] the development of species may not be a unique, developmental affair at all but may have occurred innumerable times with similar but not identical results. If we could look back far enough in the zoologic book of fossils, we might find the footprints of the Archangel Gabriel coming before the protozoic beginnings to which evolutionary philosophers like Herbert Spencer are so devoted.

2. EVOLUTION AND NATURAL SELECTION

Wright analyzed the logical structure of evolutionary thought in his articles on "The Limits of Natural Selection," "The Genesis of Species" and "Evolution by Natural Selection," all of which appeared in the *North American Review* in the early 1870's. Wright called these articles his definition and defense of

Darwinism.[16] Since he was answering specific objections, he wrote in a piecemeal and detailed manner. However, the following three general points manage to catch the flavor and purpose of his rambling essays.

(a) At the outset, Wright objected to the term evolutionary theory.[17] The word theory in science—as used, for example, in the phrase "the kinetic theory of gases"—refers either to a physical model or to a law that has explanatory value. Evolution, however, does not explain anything; it requires explanation itself. Hence, it is not a theory. Darwin's concept of natural selection explains how the evolution of species came about; hence it is legitimately called a theory.

Wright warned that one should not expect the explanatory power of natural selection to be as great as physical concepts like acceleration, momentum and force.[18] The concept of natural selection is used to explain a concrete series of events, the origin of species—not a highly controlled and artificial series of events in a laboratory. Admittedly the study of plants and animals under domestication might be interpreted as a controlled study; but even if one thus successfully discovered biological laws of a Galilean type, their application to the concrete course of evolution would still be difficult and imprecise—just as the geophysicist's application of physical laws to uncontrolled nature is difficult and imprecise. Wright also compared the explanatory power of natural selection to the laws of political economy. Knowing these laws, one still cannot explain accurately or in detail the actual establishment of prices in the market —not only because the laws are not sufficiently detailed but also because the concrete course of events is too complex.

(b) The concept of natural selection, Wright said, is briefly this: the characteristics of a species vary minutely in every possible way among the individuals of a species. Some of these minute variations, by chance, successfully adapt the individuals having them to a particular environment. Hence these individuals survive, passing along these characteristics to their progeny. In this way, these minute variations, which themselves vary indefinitely, are naturally selected. Darwin, Wright observed,[19] called the appearance of minute variations accidental, by which he meant that their appearances could not be predicted or explained by the genetic knowledge available at the time. He certainly did not mean that these variations were uncaused. Yet, Wright averred, the Jesuit naturalist St. George Mivart did so interpret him.

> Mr. Mivart, like many another writer, seems to forget the age of the world in which he lives and for which he writes—the age of "experimental philosophy," the very standpoint of which, its fundamental assumption, is the universality of physical causation. . . . As if to the physical philosopher there could possibly be an absolute and distinct class, not included under the law of causation, "that every event must have a cause. . . ."[20]

In the middle of his discussion of natural selection Wright is thus surprisingly plunged into the middle of a general and perplexing philosophical problem. Unfortunately he does not give his best performances in this discussion. He offers two reasons for accepting the belief that every event has a cause, but neither explanation is very convincing.

First, Wright suggests that this law of causation is an inductive generalization.[21] We discover that w, x, y and z have causes and so conclude that all events have causes—just as we discover, presumably, that swans w, x, y and z are white and so conclude that all swans are white. But this reason for accepting the law will not do. The analogy breaks down; for, after all, black swans are known to exist. Certainly Wright did not want to admit even the *possibility* that uncaused events might be discovered. Wright sensed such objections, no doubt, since he quickly gave another reason.

The law of causality, Wright said, is a *presupposition* of scientific inquiry. "The very hope of experimental philosophy . . . is based on . . . the *a priori* presumption that physical causation is universal; that the constitution of nature is written in its actual manifestations, and needs only to be deciphered by experimental and inductive research. . . ."[22] What Wright had in mind was this: it would be pointless for a person to look for something unless he were willing to assume that the thing exists. It would be just as pointless for a scientist to look for causes unless he were willing to assume that they always existed. He presumes that every event has a cause in order to make the search for them sensible. But this reason for accepting the law of causation also encounters difficulties. No doubt it would be silly to look for causes if one did not presume that *some* events had them. But this presumption is all one needs to make the quest for causes sensible. One might believe that events in chemistry are caused and

hence look for their causes while believing that
events in biology are uncaused and hence not in-
vestigate in this area at all. As a recent commentator
has observed, "Failure and despair in some cases
are compatible with optimism and success in
others."[23]

(c) Wright analyzed the concept of species in
some detail, and it was this analysis that particularly
pleased Darwin. Darwin's contemporaries intimated
that J. L. R. Agassiz' theory of the species was real,
fundamental and absolute, while Darwin's own view
of the species classification was conventional, arbitrary and relative. Darwin did not like this description of his view but was unable to put his finger on
what was wrong with it. Consequently, he was quite
pleased when Wright came to his aid.

According to Wright,[24] classes or species of anything may be labeled real or fundamental when the
individuals composing the class have a cluster of
characteristics in common. On the other hand, a
class may be said to be conventional or arbitrary
when the individuals composing the class have only
the characteristics in common which formed the
basis of classification. Thus the class of mammals is
a real or fundamental class, while the class of individuals composed of people whose last names begin
with the letters A through D is a conventional or
arbitrary species.

However, Wright pointed out, sometimes a second
ingredient is added to the characterization of a real
or fundamental class, namely, that the individuals
composing the class exhibit precisely the same set
of characteristics throughout all time. Logicians
called this ingredient "the immutability of species."
This notion was usually the one people had in mind

when they said that real classes are absolute. Darwin, Wright continued, did not view species as immutable or absolute. In *this* sense his species concept is not real or fundamental. On the other hand, even for Darwin, the individuals in a class at any given time continue to exhibit clusters of characteristics, albeit the characteristics exhibited slowly change. In *this* sense his classes *are* real or fundamental. Critics of Darwin, who did not make the crucial distinction between the two senses of the words real and fundamental, erroneously viewed Darwin's concept of species as altogether conventional and arbitrary.

Darwin was so pleased to have the critics set straight on this and other matters that he reprinted Wright's article on "The Genesis of Species" and distributed it in England.[25] Perhaps his English colleagues, who would not dream of reading an American periodical, might be enlightened in spite of themselves.

3. TWO KINDS OF EXPLANATION

An unusual aspect of Wright's philosophy of science is his distinction between two different kinds of scientific explanation. This distinction also proved useful in his discussions of several traditional philosophical problems. As we shall see, he relied on it in his discussions of emergence, determinism and materialism.

According to Wright,[26] one way of explaining an event is to state the cause of its occurrence. For example, one explains the falling of a stone by saying that it was left unsupported above the surface of the earth. However, the nature of this cause is wholly unlike the nature of its effect. There is nothing in the notion of being unsupported that suggests (in an *a priori* way) falling. One simply has to *experience* their constant conjunction and hence conclude that they are causally related.

The second way of explaining an event is to state the cause of its occurrence and, at the same time, to analyze or decompose it into its constituents. Wright said that this sort of explanation is the most perfect and occurs only in mechanics. The parallelogram of forces might be a good example of what he had in mind. Consider the following figure.

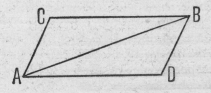

An object moves from A to B. One explains this movement by saying that the object was acted upon by a force which would at the end of a second carry it to C. At the same time it was also acted on by a force which would at the end of a second carry it to D. The result of the two forces is to carry the object to the point B, such that ABCD is a parallelogram, as in the figure. Hence one has explained the effect by giving the conditions of its occurrence, the action of the two forces, and has analyzed the effect into its constituents (A-B is the result of an A-C and an A-D constituent). In this most perfect sort of explanation there is nothing new in the result; it is a sum of its constituents. Moreover, given the mechanical notions of force A-C and force A-D, one knows immediately that A-B will occur. He does not have to experience its conjunction with the other events. It *must* occur. The reason it *must* occur is precisely that there is nothing new in this effect.

(a) *Emergence*. Wright never actually used the word emergence, but his concept of two different kinds of explanation constitutes a kind of embryonic emergentist view. The doctrine of emergence, favored by the well-known philosophers Samuel Alexander, Lloyd Morgan and Henri Bergson, is not always clear, but one feature is always present—some properties and events in the world arise suddenly and unexpectedly. Their first appearance could not be predicted from a knowledge of previous events, no matter how complete such knowledge might be. These properties or events, then, are new or novel. "These properties are emergents, not resultants."[27]

Wright, of course, had already expressed the first part of the emergence viewpoint: many elements of the world are unexpected in the sense that their first appearance could not be predicted. Only the events in mechanics for which a perfect explanation is possible can have their first appearance predicted. Other events can be predicted only after they recur numerous times. In the following quotation Wright reiterates this view and explicitly commits himself to the position that such events are new or novel:

Experimental science, as in chemistry, is full of examples of the discovery of new properties or new powers, which, so far as the conditions of their appearances were previously known, did not follow from antecedent conditions, except in an incidental manner—that is, in a manner *not then foreseen* to be involved in them; and these effects became afterwards predictable from what had become known to be their antecedent conditions only by the empirical laws or rules which inductive experimentation had established.[28]

Moreover, "according to the theory of evolution, new uses of old powers arise discontinuously both in the bodily and mental natures of the animal. . . ."[29]

These lines, and others of Wright's which suggest the emergence view, had an influence far beyond anything he might have expected. After Wright's death Samuel Alexander was poking around a secondhand bookstall in London and came across a copy of Wright's *Philosophical Discussions*.[30] He was more than a little impressed with it and projected ideas like Wright's into his own full-blown doctrine of emergence. But Wright would not have approved this destiny of his little idea, for Alexander even had God as an emergent event.

(b) *Determinism*. Wright, as we have seen, believed that every event has a cause. Charles Sanders Peirce called this view universal determinism or necessitarianism. He characterized it in the following way.[31] If one knew all the laws of the universe and knew the exact state of the universe at any moment, then he could predict the occurrence of every subsequent event in the universe and could predict every characteristic of these events. But if this universal determinism were true, he continued, then there would be no novelty in the universe; everything to come is built in, so to speak, from the beginning. But, clearly, there is novelty in the universe; hence universal determinism must be wrong.

Wright had no difficulty in meeting Peirce's ob-

jection to his view. The determinist does not claim,
as Peirce thought, that if he had sufficient knowledge
he could predict the first occurrence and the characteristics of every event. He claims that this sort of
prediction occurs only for certain events in mechanics. The first occurrences of most events—to say
nothing of their characteristics—cannot be predicted;
hence such events and characteristics are genuinely
new or novel. Consequently, Peirce's argument collapses since one can be a determinist and still account
for novelty. But, one might argue, even though the
determinist can account for novelty, he still has a
difficulty. Since he believes that all events are caused,
he still has to believe that everything is built in from
the beginning. Wright would answer, "There was no
beginning!" Moreover:

> The appearance of a really new power in *na-*
> *ture* . . . the power of flight in the first birds, for
> example, is only involved potentially in previous
> phenomena. In the same way, no act of self-
> consciousness, however elementary, may have been
> realized before man's first self-conscious act in the
> animal world; yet the act may have been involved
> potentially in pre-existing powers or causes. The
> derivation of this power, supposing it to have been
> observed by a finite angelic . . . intelligence, could
> not have been foreseen to be involved in the men-
> tal causes, on the conjunction of which it might,
> nevertheless, have been seen to depend.[32]

(c) *Materialism*. James McCosh, a Scottish philosopher who became President of Princeton in 1869,
ascribed to the materialist (by which term he meant
anyone who did not believe in God) the view that

aggregated atoms, dancing at will and by chance, could produce the fancies of Shakespeare, the sub-limities of Milton and the moral grandeur of Soc-rates.[33] Since intelligible results could not come from chaotic origins, argued McCosh, the materialist is mistaken.

Wright, never impressed with McCosh, thought this argument pointless because he saw no reason whatever for accepting the idea of an atomic chaos.[34] Through the years, he declared, philosophers have been hoodwinked by Anaxagoras' introducing *nous,* an independent agency of intelligence, into the world. They have simply assumed that anything other than *nous* must be chaotic and have no coherence or law-fulness of its own. But atomic particles *do* exhibit their own orderliness. Moreover, Wright continued, McCosh's argument is utterly loose and vague. He says that atomic particles do not have the power to produce human genius. But why not? Presumably because physical causes which have no element of consciousness or intelligence cannot give rise to effects which do exhibit such characteristics. But such a claim, Wright said, depends upon the mistaken belief that a cause cannot give rise to new or novel characteristics in its effects.

McCosh also charged the materialist with believing that if one knew enough about the collocations and movements of atoms, he could predict and explain the affection of a mother for her son, of a patriot for his country and of a Christian for his Saviour.[35] This talk is loose indeed, Wright felt, but McCosh appar-ently intended to say that the materialist believes that if he knew enough about the physical world, he could predict the occurrence and characteristics of all rational and volitional behavior. However, Wright pointed out, no materialist, nor any determinist, would dream of making such a sweeping claim.[36] A materialist and a determinist like himself held that a completely detailed knowledge of the physical world would allow one to predict the first occurrence and characteristics of only a few events. To be sure, all events are caused, but many events and characteristics are, nevertheless, novel and unique.

Chapter 5

PERENNIAL PROBLEMS

Left to his own devices, Wright probably would have written nothing. He needed the spur of controversy to bring him to his desk. Let someone misrepresent or misunderstand some point, and he was quick to reply. Indeed most of his work, with the major exception of "The Evolution of Self-Consciousness," is polemical. Wright fought his hardest and happiest battles over the perennially fascinating problems in general philosophy: What is the relation between common-sense knowledge and philosophical beliefs? Is *a priori* knowledge possible? What is the meaning of the concept cause? What is the nature of space—infinite or bounded? What is the nature of physical objects? The present chapter will examine his answers to the first four questions; the following chapter, his answer to the last one.

1. THE ROLE OF COMMON SENSE

Wright ascribed to Scottish philosophers like Thomas Reid, Dugald Stewart, and James McCosh complete disdain for such philosophical statements as "Time is unreal" or "There are no physical objects."[1] Such statements, they argued, blatantly fly in the face of common sense. They must be mistaken, for they entail the falsity of statements in ordinary life that we know to be true. If time is unreal, then it is false that time measures anything. If there are no physical objects, then it is false that John stubbed his toe on a stone. But since we experience the passing of time and we see John stub his toe on the stone, we know that the statements about them are true.

Wright strenuously rejected the Scottish view that philosophical statements like "There are no physical objects" contradict common-sense knowledge.[2] When the idealist philosopher says "There are no physical objects" he means that there are no physical substances which exist when unperceived, but he does not mean that there are no stones, trees or lamp posts in the ordinary sense. Of course there are stones. Here is one, and it is just what it is experienced to be, hard, brown, round and so on. A stone, like any physical object, is simply a cluster of sensations. The idealist, in short, does not deny the truth of common-sense statements about physical objects but suggests what he thinks the words physical object should rightly mean, namely, cluster of sensations. In Wright's words, ". . . the idealist does not deny that there is an existence properly enough called the external world, but he wishes to ascertain the nature of this reality by studying what the notion of externality really implies. . . ."[3] In another place he said, "Does Idealism deny that there are such objects? Is not its doctrine rather a definition of the nature of these objects than a denial of their existence?" Moreover, "there is nothing in positive science, or the study of phenomena and their laws, which Idealism conflicts with. . . . Astronomy is just as real a science, as true an account of phenomena and their laws, if phenomena are only mental states, as on the other theory."[4] Indeed, Wright said, no philosopher wishes to deny either common sense or scientific truths; philosophers happily accept them as *true* but wonder what precisely their fundamental concepts *mean*. "As if truths were on trial for their lives! As if the 'sceptic' desired worse of them than their better acquaintance!"[5]

Wright's distinction between believing a statement to be true, on the one hand, and knowing clearly the meaning of it, on the other, has a decided modern ring to it. In modern terms, one could make the same point in the following way. The job of the philosopher is to explain the meaning of a concept like physical object by providing its *analysis*. The new concept that analysis provides, however, must meet this requirement: it must be substitutable for the original one in such a way that any true sentence in which the original one occurs remains true after the substitution. For example, if the sentence "John stubbed his toe on a stone" is true, then the sentence "John stubbed his toe on a hard, round, brown cluster of sensations" must also be true. Nowadays this view is shared by many philosophers, otherwise quite different, who come under the general rubric of analytical philosophy. So Wright's clear perception that the task of the philosopher is not to deny the truth of common-sense knowledge is an important prefigurement of the spirit of much modern philosophy.[6]

2. IS *a priori* KNOWLEDGE POSSIBLE?

Wright did not believe that *a priori* knowledge is possible. To appreciate his view we need to know specifically what Immanuel Kant meant by this term, because it was this eighteenth-century German philosopher whom Wright had in mind whenever he wrote about the possibility of *a priori* knowledge.[7]

Kant distinguished three kinds of statements—synthetic, analytic and synthetic *a priori*. A synthetic statement makes a factual-like claim and is known to be true or false only through experience. "All bachelors are lonely" would be an example of a synthetic statement. An analytic statement asserts nothing about the world and is known to be true, so to speak, by its form alone. "All bachelors are unmarried," is one example of an analytic statement; it tells us nothing about bachelors since "unmarried male" is the *definition* of bachelor. Moreover, one does not learn the truth of this statement through experience; one knows it is necessarily true because it simply announces what is definitionally true.

A synthetic *a priori* statement, the controversial one, asserts something about the world, is not definitionally true, but nevertheless is necessarily true. One of Kant's examples of a synthetic *a priori* statement is $7+5=12$.[8] Kant argued that the notion of being equal to 12 is not contained in the notions of 7 and 5, and hence the judgment is synthetic. But it is, of course, necessarily true and not known through experience. In geometry, Kant said, the notion of straight does not imply that of shortest; hence the statement "a straight line is the shortest distance between two points" is synthetic. But, again, it is necessarily true and not known through experience.

Convinced that synthetic *a priori* knowledge does exist, Kant tried to explain how it is possible. Take the case of space. Everything that we experience is in space. It is impossible to think of an experience not occurring in space. The notion of space and its properties, then, cannot be learned from experience because it is presupposed in every experience. Since the notion of space is a pre-condition of experience, the mind of the perceiver must impose the spatial form on the content of experience. Thus every experience not only comes in spatial patterns but *must* do so. Thus, also, geometrical truths like "a straight line is the shortest distance between two points," since they specify the spatial characteristics that the mind imposes on the world of experience, *must* be true of the world of experience. They are, in short, synthetic *a priori* truths.

Wright did not believe in the existence of synthetic *a priori* knowledge; hence he disallowed the need to show how it is possible.[9] He believed that all the alleged examples of *a priori* statements are either disguised analytic or synthetic statements. In the geometrical cases, Wright had a difficult time. He admitted that such statements are necessarily true, but he believed that he could give an empirical or factual interpretation of this necessity. Two properties, he said, are necessarily related if they not only always occur together but also if they could not conceivably, under any conditions, occur apart.[10] The spatial properties related in geometrical statements are necessary in this sense: we not only always experience them together but we cannot conceive of any conditions where they would not occur together.

Wright's rebuttal of the geometry cases is weak, of course, for conceivability is a relative matter. What people find conceivable and inconceivable is a function of what they already know. At one time it was inconceivable that people could remain at the antipodes for they would fall off the earth unless their feet were glued down! But now it is perfectly conceivable. At one time it was inconceivable that under any conditions a straight line might not be the shortest distance between two points, yet the advent of non-Euclidean geometries (and their later interpretation) provided just such conditions. But Wright's answer was no worse, if no better, than those given by other nineteenth-century empirical or positivistic philosophers. Kant's geometrical cases gave them all a bad time. They admitted that geometry said something about the world, yet it apparently was necessarily true. Only later did empiricists discover a better answer to Kant than the sort of answer Wright offered. They distinguished two different types of geometry: mathematical and applied, or, as is sometimes said, pure and applied. They interpreted the expressions of mathematical geometry as analytic truths and interpreted the statements of applied geometry as the probably true statements of empirical science.

While Wright disbelieved in synthetic *a priori* knowledge, and hence in Kant's explanation of its possibility, he believed nevertheless that the mind of the perceiver does impose forms on experience in some empirical way. A person would not perceive the color red, for example, unless the form of previous experiences imposed itself on the content of the present experience. We only perceive a color, Wright said, "by rousing all the colors of memory which similitude or contrast can by association connect with it."[11] If there were no such unconscious comparison of the present sensation with other previous similar and dissimilar ones, then there would be no grounds for seeing red. "Red" refers to far more than a present sensation. "For what is it in the intuition [sensation] which is cognizable, unless it be its likeness or unlikeness to other intuitions?"[12]

The same analysis applies to the perception of relations. One perceives the book *on* the table because he recognizes it as similar to previous experiences of x being *on* y—the hat on the head, the book on the shelf, the inkstand on the table, and so on. The perceptions of properties and relations, Wright continued, are like the operations of intellect.

Instead of allowing two orders of independent cognitions, those of the senses and those of the intellect, I would maintain that all cognitions alike involve understanding in some degree, or some relation of the new impression to the previous content of the mind. An impression is cognized only when brought into consciousness; that is, into relations with what we have previously thought or felt or desired.[13]

According to Wright, the forming aspect of experience operates in two ways. The previous experience of any individual operates as a forming element to all subsequent experiences of this individual. But some time or other in the experience of any individual there must be some first perceptual experience which could not have any forming element functioning for it. Wright suggested that an individual brings to such first experiences an inherited backlog of similar and dissimilar cases and the inherited capacity to relate his own first experiences to the proper cases.[14]

3. THE MEANING OF "CAUSE"

Wright defended David Hume's analysis of the concept of cause.[15] Hume believed that the way to discover the meaning of the notion cause is to inquire into the manner by which sentences using this concept are *verified*. How does one check the truth of the sentence "Eating strawberries is the cause of my rash"? He would check the food eaten at every meal prior to the occurrence of the rash. If he could show that every time the rash appeared he had eaten strawberries previously, and that strawberries were the only food of which he could say this, then he would have good reason for saying that "Eating strawberries is the cause of my rash." Or if he could show that he ate two meals, identical in every way except that at the first he ate strawberries and at the second he did not eat strawberries and that after the first the rash occurred while after the second it did not, then, again, he would have good reason for saying that "Eating strawberries is the cause of my rash." Hume inquired then into the feature which is common to these different ways of showing the truth of any sentence using the word cause. He concluded that the feature is *constant conjunction*. Whenever one event occurs, another one, and only one, does also. Since this is the only evidence one ever has for saying that anything causes anything else, then he can only mean by the notion of cause that two things always go together—or, as Hume said, the two things are in constant conjunction.[16]

Wright, however, was troubled by Thomas Reid's objection that simple constant conjunction is not an adequate definition of cause because we can find instances of events which are constantly conjoined but nevertheless not causally related. Night follows day and day follows night constantly, Reid observed, but no one would dream of saying that either one is the cause of the other.

Wright concluded that Hume's view must be supplemented in some way to avoid Reid's criticism.[17] In order for two events to be causally related, he said, they must not only be constantly conjoined but unconditionally conjoined. According to Wright, if two events are causally related, this means

that the truth they predicate is unconditional—is independent of any other facts; that there exists nothing to prevent the thing from being, or being so and so; or that the particular fact does not depend on any conditions which we can suppose from the evidence of experience to be variable.[18]

What Wright had in mind is this: we do not believe, for example, that night is the cause of day or vice versa because we can easily imagine variable conditions under which the phenomenon would not occur. Given a ball twirling on its own axis around a candle, it is easy to see that the sequences of dark and light would be interrupted by placing a screen between the ball and candle. In the same way we can easily imagine a cosmic screen obtruding between the sun and earth, and in this way the sequence of night and day would be broken down. To be sure, we cannot actually erect a cosmic screen and observe the breakdown of the heretofore constant conjunction, but we can *conceive in principle* the conditions under which it would break down. This conception is enough to show that the sequence is not unconditional and hence fails to qualify as a causal sequence. Thus Reid's counterexample is not a valid one and fails any longer to count seriously as a criticism of Hume's analysis of cause.

Wright's reply to Reid's objection is also effective against a criticism of Hume's view made by William James.[19] According to James, one who held Hume's view could not distinguish between real and apparent causes. To make his point, he recalled an experience which he had while riding on a train. Every time the train stopped, the smoke from the stove in his coach flooded out and almost suffocated the passengers. Whenever the train moved, the smoke disappeared. At one stop James asked the conductor if anything could be done about the smoke. The conductor replied that he should wait until the train started and the smoke would disappear. Since he had experienced a constant conjunction between the moving of the train and the disappearance of the smoke, he had concluded that the former caused the latter. But, James said, we know that the moving of the train is only the *apparent* cause of the disappearance of the smoke, not the *real* cause. The moving of the train caused a draft which produced a vacuum in the smoke stack so the smoke could ascend, and this event is the real cause of the disappearance of the smoke. Wright's reply to Reid, of course, is applicable again. One who holds Hume's view would not accept the constant conjunction of moving train and disappearance of smoke as a causal relation at all because he could easily conceive of conditions under which the constant conjunction would break down. For example, one might leave a lid on the smoke stack while the train moved.

The critics of Hume, Wright felt, generally make the mistake of trying to explain why events are constantly conjoined. There is a power in the cause, they say, which *makes* the effect occur; and this causal power explains why the two events are constantly conjoined. Such an explanation, Wright said, is neither reasonable nor required.[20] There is only one possible kind of answer to the question "Why are events constantly conjoined?" Two events *must* be so related if their correlation can be deduced from higher-order laws of nature. However, science has its ultimate laws for which there is no such explanation and for which it is inappropriate to ask for any explanation. Ultimate laws, like the law of gravity, also correlate types of events, but these ultimate correlations cannot themselves be explained. Such laws manifest the hard core of reality which simply is—a brute fact of nature. According to Wright:

Metaphysics demands, in the interest of mystery, [to know] *why* an elementary antecedent is followed by its elementary consequent. But this question does not arise from that inquisitiveness which inspires scientific research. It is asked to show that it cannot be answered, and hence that all science rests on mystery. . . . But, being a question, it is open to answer; or it makes legitimate, at least, the counterquestion, When can a question be properly asked? or, What is the purpose of asking a question? Is it not to discover the causes, classes, laws, or rules that determine the existence, properties, or production of a thing or event? . . . The highest generality, or universality, in the elements or connections of elements in phenomena, is the utmost reach both in the power and the desire of the scientific intellect. Explanation cannot go, and does not rationally seek to go, beyond such facts. The invention of noumena to account for ultimate and universal properties and relations in phenomena arises from no other necessity than the action of a desire urged beyond the normal promptings of its power.[21]

4. THE NATURE OF SPACE

Wright believed that it is impossible to know whether space has boundaries or is infinite in extent. He believed that this question, like certain other philosophical ones, is a closed question.[22] By a closed question he meant one where we are ignorant beyond the possibility of enlightenment. Most metaphysical questions, he thought, are closed in this sense because there is no way in which experience, the only legitimate source of knowledge, can resolve the questions. He argued effectively in his articles and letters against Sir William Hamilton's and Francis E. Abbot's efforts to show that some answer *can* be given to the question "Is space bounded or infinite?"

Taking space as a whole, Hamilton said, it must be either bounded or infinite (or, as he put it, limited or unlimited).[23] Since these notions are contradictories, one must be true and the other false. But, he continued, the notion of bounded space is inconceivable because no one can think of any extent of space except as contained within a still larger extent of space, and so on *ad infinitum*. But the notion of infinite space is also inconceivable because we can magnify our imagination of space at will and still not achieve one atom of the infinite. However, Hamilton concluded, since the two notions are contradictories, space *must* be either bounded or infinite. Thus, one of two alternatives, neither of which can be conceived as possible, must nevertheless be the case.

Hamilton generalized cases like that of space into his famous "Law of the Conditioned," according to which, all that can be positively thought "lies between two opposite poles of thought, which, as exclusive of each other, cannot, on the principles of identity and contradiction, both be true, but of which, on the principle of excluded middle, the one or the other must."[24] Hamilton concluded that a second-order kind of metaphysical knowledge is possible: while we can only know the conditioned which lies between the two metaphysical inconditionates, nevertheless we can know that one of these inconditionates must be true.

Wright criticized Hamilton's analysis of space and his law of the conditioned in two ways. First, he felt that Hamilton's use of the concept of infinite space was self-contradictory.[25] Infinite space for Hamilton is not simply the indefinite—that is, greater than any finite space; hence it must be an entity in its own right. For Hamilton, Wright said, infinite space

. . . is a unit, a whole. But it is without limits. It is, then, a whole without limits. But a whole implies limits. We know of no whole which has not limits. We can conceive of no whole which has not limits. Limits, in fact, belong to the essence of every whole of which we speak intelligibly. Does not the metaphysical idea or definition of infinity involve, therefore, a contradiction?[26]

Second, Hamilton is inconsistent, Wright averred, in yet another way. Infinite space and bounded space for Hamilton, he said, are inconditionates—that is, unknowable metaphysical alternatives. Yet he tries to prove that one inconditionate—we know not which—must be the case by applying the laws of excluded middle and noncontradiction to the two metaphysical concepts. But it is inconsistent, he concluded, to say that we have no knowledge of the inconditionates when we claim to know that the laws of thought apply to them.[27]

Wright's criticism, however, might be met in the following way. Hamilton apparently believed that any statement must have a significant negation in order to qualify as knowledge. The statement that my pencil is yellow would constitute knowledge, if it is yellow, since it could have been green or red instead. The law of noncontradiction, however, has no significant negation—indeed, it would be intellectual nihilism to deny this law by saying, for example, that it is both raining and not raining at this instant. The same is true for the law of excluded middle. Consequently, Hamilton might claim that these laws, since they do not have significant negations, can be applied to metaphysical unknowables without constituting, or resulting in, any knowledge of them. Only if one could establish that space is infinite or that space is finite would he have knowledge of these inconditionates—since these statements both have the other as a significant negation. To be sure, one might object to such a restriction on the use of the word knowledge; but, given this use of the word, Hamilton would be perfectly consistent in claiming that the laws of excluded middle and non-contradiction apply to the inconditionates, and yet we have no knowledge of them.

In spite of his criticisms of Hamilton, Wright still had a lingering affection for his work, and he wanted to see it done full justice. He defended his early master on several counts against criticisms by J. S. Mill and Francis E. Abbot, a good friend of Wright and occasional visitor at the Metaphysical Club. Abbot had criticized the law of the conditioned in the following way.[28] Hamilton said that two unknowable inconditionates like infinite space and finite space are contradictories; that is, one must be true and the other false. Yet the conditioned, the actual positive experience of space (such as things *in* space and spatial relations like "to the right of"), is the mean between these two unknowable inconditionates. Abbot thought Hamilton here misused the notion of contradictories and the mean. Certainly if the two inconditionates are really contradictories they are mutually exclusive and exhaustive so there could be no third alternative or mean—the conditioned—between them.

Wright was unconvinced by Abbot's criticism.[29] Hamilton, he said, never intended the conditioned, or positive knowledge, to be a logical mean between two metaphysical extremes. Rather, he thought of any positive knowledge lying between two metaphysical extremes as a kind of psychological mean. From this psychological mean, one struggled, unsuccessfully, to achieve knowledge of one of the metaphysical extremes. "These acts, inasmuch as they are irrelevant extensions of sensuous images, are in a psychological sense opposed to the logical extremes because they are in principle incapable of comprehending them. But this does not mean that it is

logically a third alternative in opposition to the inconditionates."[30] Since it is not a logical third alternative, Wright concluded that Hamilton does not vio-
late the notion of contradictories, or the law of excluded middle. Wright is probably correct in his defense of Hamilton; for, after all, the point of
Hamilton's law of the conditioned is to demonstrate
that our inability to conceive something as existing
is no sign of its actual nonexistence. Indeed, we can
prove that one of two metaphysical truths must be
the case, but we struggle in vain with the knowable
to discover which one it is.

Wright presented his positive views on space in an
interesting series of letters to Abbot, written during
the latter part of the 1860's.[31] Empirically, Wright
said, the notion of space arises by the perception of
spatial relations. We see that x is *above* y, x is *to the
right of* y, x is *in front of* y, and so on. These relations, he said, are as directly experienced as simple
properties like red, sour, and B-flat. It is only by an
abstractive set that a person attends separately to
related objects and thus sees them "out of the relation which is as much in the sensuous intuition of
them as their colors or shapes."[32] He felt that Abbot
was wrong in believing that a person perceives properties through his sense organs but sees relations only through an intellectual act of understanding.

To explain what we do experience—namely, objects in spatial relations—we must, Wright admitted, pass beyond experience.[33] We must assume that
space is continuous, that is, extends beyond our perceptual apprehension. Wright believed that his assumption "Space is continuous," unlike metaphysical
views of space, was simply an empirical notion which
had to be assumed in order to explain the possibility

of what we do experience, namely, a multitude of objects spatially related. Wright's disclaimer of metaphysical import, however, seems unconvincing since the hypothesis "Space is continuous" is not justified by evidence in the way that scientific hypotheses are. Rather it must be justified, if at all, in the same way that metaphysical claims about the infinity or finitude of space are justified, namely, by philosophical argument. According to Wright, the question whether space is infinite or finite would be a closed question because it is incapable of a sensory answer, but the same would be true also for his own view that space is continuous.

Even if it is in some sense metaphysical, Wright was convinced that the notion "Space is continuous" is superior to the views that it is bounded or that it is infinite.[34] In the first place, the philosophical arguments which purport to prove that space is infinite or bounded never fail to be unconvincing, as we saw in the case of Hamilton. In the second place, "Space is continuous" is the simplest and least controversial assumption one has to make in order to explain the possibility of what we do experience. Wright wrote:

Infinite space, as an hypothesis to account for anything of which we are truly cognizant, not only transcends our powers of conception, but also the necessities of thought. A simpler hypothesis is competent to do all that it can do. We need only space which includes all that we can know, and extends beyond our powers of knowing or conceiving it.[35]

What, finally, did Wright think of the likely success of his arguments against the metaphysical notions of bounded and infinite space? His hopes were not high. The conflict between metaphysical and positive philosophies, he said, appears unavoidable and endless. "Deathless warriors, irreconcilable and alternately victorious, according to the nature of the ground, or to advantages of position, continually re-new their struggles along the line of development in each individual mind and character."[36] Wright often returned to this notion that our philosophies are func-tions of our different characters. We have certain ends-in-view at the beginning of our philosophical in-quiry and search around simply for justifications of our predilections. Wright asserted this view, however, not in anything like an absolute sense. Philosophies, he thought, are subtle combinations of genuine phil-osophical justification, on the one hand, and ration-alization of predilections, on the other—and who is to tell, he might have added in his whimsical way, which will get us to the truth quicker? In any case, William James was impressed again by Wright's thought and later formulated his own version of it by saying that philosophers are born either tough or tender-minded and philosophize accordingly.[37]

Chapter 6

PHYSICAL OBJECTS

How do we know that we get reliable information about physical objects through perception? This question has long intrigued philosophers, and Wright was no exception. His examination of this problem was longer and more sustained than any other he ever made. He devoted attention to it in his long monograph "The Evolution of Self-Consciousness" —the least polemical and most involved of all his essays—and he considered it in passing in many other contexts. From all these sources we are able to reconstruct in detail Wright's views about the nature of physical objects.

1. THE OLD VIEWS

At first glance there seems to be no puzzle about our knowledge of physical objects. I see physical objects and never doubt that they exist or have the properties they appear to have. This common-sense view is called naïve realism. But it immediately runs into difficulties. What we perceive is dependent in some sense on the nature of our sense organs. What we take to be the nature and properties of physical objects may simply be pinned onto whatever is out there by our way of perceiving. What if one's eyes were constructed differently? Would he not have a totally different picture of what physical objects are like? A horse's eye is different from the human eye; it probably lacks depth vision. Thus the physical objects of a horse's vision are quite different from those in our world! Moreover, we know that some aspects of physical objects we do not see at all. Bees see ultraviolet light, but man does not. Imagine all the other aspects of physical reality which may pass him by.

There is further difficulty with the view of naive realism. Since we have illusions and hallucinations sometimes, it is clear that our senses can deceive us. One perceives a stick submerged in water as bent, but this perception is illusory, we say, for the stick is really straight. Hence one wrongly perceives a property of a physical object. One sees an oasis in the desert; but this perception is hallucinatory, we say, for there is no such place or object at all.

Illusions and hallucinations show us that we are deceived some of the time about the nature of physical objects; but perhaps we are deceived *all* of the time. The only way that I know a perception is illusory is by accepting a subsequent perception as veridical. I thought the suit was black but in stronger light I see it is blue. The only way I know the black perception was illusory is by accepting the later blue perception as veridical. But what right do I have to assume this? Perhaps this subsequent perception is itself illusory, as some still later perception might show. And so on *ad infinitum*. If some later perception does not show it to be illusory, perhaps I simply have not waited long enough. The point, in short, is that I can never know for certain that I have a veridical perception and hence correctly apprehend the nature of physical objects.

Of all these traditional criticisms of naïve realism,

Wright particularly urged the importance of illusions and hallucinations.[1] The inability to account for these perceptual difficulties, he felt, effectively removed this so-called common-sense viewpoint from serious philosophical consideration. As we shall see, he was equally skeptical about the conclusions which were drawn from these criticisms under the name of representative realism.

According to the representative realist, when a person has an illusion he does not perceive a property of an object, but he must perceive *something*. When he has an hallucination he does not perceive an object, but he must perceive *something*. In both cases, the representative realist says, we directly apprehend our own sensations and not physical objects at all.[2] The next step in his argument is to extend the claim that we directly apprehend our own sensations to *all* experience. We never directly perceive physical objects; the only things we are ever directly aware of are our own sensations. Sometimes the representative realist justifies this generalization by pointing to the scientific notion of perception.[3] In the case of seeing an object, light waves reflect off the object, impinge on the retina, excite nervous energy which travels through the afferent nerve fibers to the central nervous system, and then one sees the object. But clearly one does not really see the object. What he sees is the end product of a long causal chain—namely, his own sensations.

The representative realist concludes that physical objects are never directly experienced but that we can infer something about them because our sensations, which we do directly apprehend, represent them—hence the name of representative realism. Philosophers who hold this view differ about the way in which sensations represent the physical objects which are, so to speak, behind the scenes. Some of them believe that sensations represent physical objects as effects represent their causes. To them, nothing is known of the nature of physical objects except that they are the causes of our sensations. Other philosophers believe that some sensations represent physical objects because they *resemble* them. Such philosophers distinguish between primary and secondary properties.[4] Primary properties are solidity, extension, figure, motion and number; physical objects actually have these properties and our sensations resemble them in these respects. Secondary properties are colors, sounds, tastes and so on; physical objects do not have these properties and hence our sensations do not resemble them in these respects. While an object itself does not have the property red, the object is the partial cause of our seeing red because of the reflection of light waves off its surface.

Against representative realism, Wright had a number of objections. First of all, he said, physical objects are never directly observed. Since they are forever beyond the range of experience they are metaphysical notions. Whether such objects exist or not is a closed question—one which can not be answered in principle. Thus it is gratuitous to ask it.[5] Second, how can we say that a physical object is the *cause* of a sensation? The only admissable notion of cause, Wright felt, is Hume's: within an experience two events always occur together and never apart; hence we call the first "cause" and the second "effect." Thus one could not call physical objects and sensations causally related, since the former admittedly are never directly experienced. Third, how can we say that a physical object resembles a sensation when we never experience a physical object? Of two things in experience we can say when and how one resembles another or is different from another, but it is impossible to do either when one of the things compared is within experience and the other outside experience. For the representative realist refers to the scientific theory of perception as if it establishes that we are always directly aware of our own sensations and never directly aware of physical objects. However, as Wright pointed out, the scientist, in talking about physical objects, assumes that the objects themselves are directly experienced.[6]

The next logical step, if one abandons representative realism, is subjective idealism. According to this view, physical objects are only what they are experienced to be; a physical object is simply a cluster of sensations. A pencil is a cluster, say, of round, yellow, hard, etc., sensations. This definition of physical object entails the strange view that objects exist only when perceived. "To be is to be perceived." Thus if no one is in the adjoining room, or peeking through a window or hole in the wall, then it is incorrect to say that the desk inside the room exists. The notion that physical objects pop into and out of existence, however, is more than common sense can stand, so some subjective idealists assuage the feeling of outrage by pointing out that physical objects are always percepts in God's mind and hence continue to exist in an uninterrupted fashion. Indeed, some idealists use this whole argument just to prove that God exists. Of course, they say, it is absurd to believe that objects flit into and out of existence, so we must believe in God as a steadying influence in the universe.

The idealist, Wright felt, goes wrong in several ways. First, the subjective idealist violates his own system by bringing in God as a constant perceiver. God is just as much beyond sensory experience as the representative realist's physical object. Consequently, the concept of God is no more legitimate in an idealist system than the concept of physical object. Second, the idealist is wrong also because he defines the concept of physical object as a cluster of *actual* sensations. According to Wright, one must include in the definition a reference to *possible* sensations also.[7] We can say that a desk exists in the next room even though unperceived because it would be seen if one were to enter the room. The notion of physical object, he thought, would be defined better as "a permanent possibility of sensation." This view he took over from J. S. Mill, and it is traditionally called phenomenalism. According to this view, physical objects have just the properties and nature they are experienced to have, and hence this view avoids the realist's metaphysical notion of an unobservable physical object. It also avoids the idealist's odd notion that objects come into and go out of existence. Because it avoided both realism and idealism, Wright accepted it.

One might argue against phenomenalism in the following way.[8] There was a world with physical objects in it long before there were any animals, to say nothing of human beings, of whom we could say, "If they were to go and look, then they would see such and such an object." Wright, however, was not impressed by this argument.[9] However unfit the world may be at any time for the existence of an animal body with perceptive organs, it is never unfit to be perceived had a perceiver existed. Rather than an argument against phenomenalism, this notion points up nicely the concept of possibility which is at the heart of the phenomenalist view. According to the phenomenalist, Wright said, the notion of physical object is dependent on the *possibility* of perception, whatever the present actualities at any time happen to be.

Although Wright accepted Mill's phenomenalism in early years, he later passed quietly beyond it into a more subtle view of phenomenalism which has come to be called neutral monism. He presents this new view in his essay on self-consciousness.

2. THE NEW VIEW

Mill's phenomenalism, after all, is not far from idealism; it simply interprets physical objects as possible sensations instead of actual ones. The word sensation still suggests that physical objects are mental in nature. Wright's neutral monism avoided this suggestion entirely.

According to Wright, ultimate reality is neutral in nature.[10] The whole class of things we directly apprehend—a loud noise, a square shape, an acrid odor, etc.—are neutral phenomena, neither mental nor physical in nature. (Sensing a noise is, no doubt, mental, but the noise sensed is a neutral phenomenon.) Neutral phenomena, it is true, do eventually become classified into mental or physical; e.g., a loud noise becomes a sensation and a square shape becomes a physical object. But such classification grows out of experience itself and has no philosophical significance. Thus where we *do* call a neutral phenomenon mental or physical, these designations are practical or functional in nature, not metaphysical.[11] Neutral phenomena remain the only ultimately real elements of our world.

In his essay on "The Evolution of Self-Consciousness" Wright explained in detail how he thought the distinction between thought and things, or the mental and physical, arises in human experience.[12] Using Darwinian concepts he showed how simple responses to signs, such as expecting rain from certain cloud patterns, could develop into full-fledged reasoning with general statements and headings. This development is crucial: the person now realizes that the memory images of clouds in the major heading "Whenever clouds of such and such shape appear, rain will follow" and the present perception of *this cloud* both signify rain.

> . . . and the contrast of thoughts [memory images] and things [present perceptions], at least in their power of suggesting that of which they may be coincident signs, could, for the first time, be perceptible. This would plant the germ of the distinctively human form of self-consciousness.[13]

If the distinction between thoughts and things, or the mental and physical, arises in this way, Wright said, it is learned or functional in nature, not intuitive or metaphysical. Thus both the realist and idealist must be wrong. According to Wright, the realist "holds that both the subject and object are absolutely, immediately, and equally known through their essential attributes in perception."[14] On the contrary, Wright felt that phenomena in the beginning were not classified as either mental or physical; they were neutral phenomena. He was willing to admit that people nowadays experience all phenomena as either mental or physical. The ability to make such classifications, he said, is, in part at least, instinctive and inherited from our ancestors.

Idealism, unlike realism, Wright said, maintains that only the conscious subject, or Self, is immediately known, and its properties are known intuitively to belong to it; but he thought this view also mistaken. "Instead of being, as the theories of idealism hold, first known as a phenomenon of the subject *ego* . . . its first unattributed condition would be, by our view, one of neutrality between the two worlds."[15]

What Wright called neutral phenomena later philosophers came to call sense-data. Sense-data are neither mental nor physical; they are whatever is sensed—a loud noise, a square shape, an acrid odor. For both Wright and present-day sense-data philosophers, a problem immediately arises. Wright dismissed naive realism because he thought it could not account for perceptual illusions and hallucinations. Can he do any better with his own view? Can the present-day sense-data theorist do any better?

Since Wright could not explain the difference between illusions and veridical perceptions as the difference between appearance and reality, between objects as they appear to us and as they really are, he must explain it as a difference among neutral phenomena themselves. Let us see how a neutral monist makes his case for illusion and hallucination, respectively.[16]

Consider the following illusion. A person is sitting in a coach car waiting for the train to start. Suddenly he feels his train moving since he sees a train passing on the next track. But it is an illusion, for it is the next train moving, not his. How does he know that it is an illusion and not a veridical perception? According to Wright, the person comes to believe his feeling of movement illusory because it does not allow a maximum amount of compatible experiences. If he were moving, then he should pass telephone poles, houses and so on, as well as the next train; but he does not. He remains stationary in respect to these other objects. Moreover, if he were moving, he could not walk to the end of the coach and descend the steps without being pitched on his head; but he discovers he can do so. The notion that the other train is moving, however, fits all of these experiences into a coherent pattern. Thus he has the right to say that his first impression was illusory and the subsequent one is the way things really are. But to Wright, "the way things really are" does not mean metaphysically real objects or states of affairs; the phrase rather designates a reliable, predictable pattern among experiences themselves. Conversely, illusion refers to an unreliable, unpredictable pattern among experiences.

Consider the following hallucination. Someone drinks too heavily and believes that there is a chair in the corner of a room, although, as a matter of fact, there is none. He may discover his hallucination by trying to sit on the chair and discovering himself sprawled on the floor. Again, one classifies the chair experience as hallucinatory because it was wild; it did not fit into a predictable pattern. Hallucination refers to a relation among experiences, just as veridical experience refers to a different sort of relation. There is no metaphysical distinction for Wright between things as they appear to be and things as they really are.[17]

Modern sense-data theorists have spent much time in discussing whether sense-data statements are certainly true or could be mistaken; and this discussion, as we shall see, throws interesting light on Wright's neutral monism. The modern sense-data theorist distinguishes between sense-data statements and physical-object statements; for example, between sentences like "This is red" and "This is a desk."[18] Physical-object statements, he says, are uncertain and subject to upset. If one says "This is a desk" he is implicitly predicting that if he moves to the other side, he will see drawers; if he sits at it, he can write; and so on. Any of these predictions may turn out to be untrue, and he can only conclude that his physical-object statement is false and that he had an illusion or hallucination.

On the other hand, sense-data theorists claim that sense-data statements like "This is red" are certainly true. To be sure, one could be linguistically mistaken in asserting a sense-datum statement. One might say "This is red" when he is not experiencing a red sense-datum at all but a blue one. In this case he simply has not learned to use the color words correctly. But sense-data statements cannot be factually mistaken. If one says "This is a blue color patch," he cannot be mistaken (except linguistically) because he does not go beyond what is given in immediate perception; he makes no implicit predictions whatsoever that might prove to be false.

Wright's view is directly opposite to most sense-data theorists. He believed that statements about neutral phenomena are no more certainly true than physical-object sentences are. Recall Wright's analysis of the empirical forming factor present in all perception, in the perception of properties and relations alike.[19] When one says "This is red," Wright claimed, he is going far beyond this one neutral phenomenon; he is comparing it with a large number of other such phenomena and judging it to be similar to certain previous ones and dissimilar to others. If we take Wright's analysis at face value, the implication is this: even statements about neutral phenomena or sense-data go beyond the particular present phenomenon and thus are not self-contained. Since one is classifying the datum, he is making a factual claim and hence could be mistaken. *This* datum may not be like others he thought it was like; hence his statement about it could be false. Hence statements about neutral phenomena would be no more certainly true than physical-object sentences are.

While Wright's view of neutral monism was new, its similarity to later views must not be exaggerated. Wright's view was transitional. As we shall see, he greatly influenced William James's formulation of a neutral position, what James called the doctrine of pure experience; and James, no doubt, influenced later philosophers. Yet, like all transitional figures, Wright not only anticipated later, more developed views but he also had strong roots in the intellectual milieu of his own day. In the present case his roots were biological. Wright believed that the ability to classify neutral phenomena into mental or physical is in part instinctive and inherited from our ancestors.[20] We can ignore Wright's biological view not only because it is dubious science but also because it is philosophically irrelevant. In spite of such nineteenth-century impedimenta and paraphernalia, the beginning of a new view about physical objects was present in Wright's work.

3. THE NOTION OF SUBSTANCE

In his essay on "The Evolution of Self-Consciousness," Wright carefully analyzed the concept of substance, claiming that it is a meaningless notion spawned by misleading sentence structure. Since the problem of substance is related closely to the problem of physical objects, it is appropriate now to examine Wright's view of substance in detail.

First, we need to be clear about the role the concept of substance plays in philosophy. Describing a pencil, one might say, "This pencil is yellow, cylindrical, smooth, hard, and so on." These predicates refer to properties or characteristics of the pencil. But, the metaphysician adds, the subject "pencil" refers to something which *has* the properties, and this something is what we mean by physical substance. Physical substance is not something observable; it is a metaphysical reality which we must assume to exist in order to explain what we do experience. What *do* we experience? Simply a cluster of properties, sensations or sense data, if you will. But these properties are properties *of* something. There must be a substance in which the properties are embedded, a substance which acts as a glue to hold the properties together so they are properties of just *this* thing. To be sure, "embedded" and "glue" are metaphors, but they are perfectly legitimate ways of making clear the rational need in this case, the assumption of a substantial reality apart from, and in addition to, the experienced properties. This assumption is one made by both the naive and representative realists.

The empiricist, on the other hand, takes an opposite view. The word pencil refers to nothing more nor less than the entire class of experienced pencil properties. In any given sentence where we predicate a property of this pencil, Wright said, the subject term refers not to a physical substance but to the whole class of pencil properties minus the one actually predicated in the sentence.[21] A pencil is a substance only in the sense that it refers to a whole group of coexisting sensations and not simply to one isolated sensation. Here the empiricist is using the same strategy as the neutral monist does in the problem of perception. Just as the word illusion does not distinguish between things as they appear to be and things as they really are but refers rather to different relations among sense-data, so the word substance does not refer to a metaphysical reality but to a specific relation among sensations (or sense data), namely, to their coexistence or clustering. Wright held precisely and completely all the empirical view we have been describing. William James gives a beautifully exact description of Wright's view:

He particularly condemned the idea of substance as a metaphysical idol. When it was objected to him that there must be some principle of oneness in the diversity of phenomena—some *glue* to hold them together and make a universe out of their mutual independence, he would reply that there is no need of a glue to join things unless we apprehend some reason why they should fall asunder. Phenomena *are* grouped—more we cannot say of them. This notion that the actuality of a thing is the absolute totality of its being was perhaps never grasped by anyone with such thoroughness as by him.[22]

Wright tried to show that the notion of substance is meaningless—or, better, confused—because it is the result of certain misleading features in the syntax of language. Wright began this part of his criticism of the concept of substance with this observation:

The languages employed by philosophers are themselves lessons in ontology, and have, in their grammatical structures, implied conceptions and beliefs common to the philosopher and to the barbarian inventors of language, as well as other implications which the former takes pains to avoid. How much besides he ought to avoid, in the correction of conceptions erroneously derived from the forms of language, is a question always important to be considered in metaphysical inquiries.[23]

The concept of substance is a good case in point. This conception, Wright said, "needs to be tested by an examination of the possible causes of it as an effect of the forms of language and other familiar associations, which, however natural, may still be misleading."[24]

The barbarian inventors of language, Wright said, did not clearly distinguish between persons and things. Indeed, they considered heavenly bodies as personal beings and fire apparently as a spirit. Thus thing words took on the function of referring to unobservable but nevertheless quite real powers that manifested themselves in various properties. Hence our syntax arose in which the subject of a sentence refers to such powerful substances and the predicate to some manifest property of it. The contrast of active and passive verbs reflects this view too.

The subject of a proposition, instead of being thought of as that vaguely determined group of phenomena with which the predicate is found to be connected, was thought either to perform an action on an object as expressed through the transitive verb, or to be acted on by the object as expressed through the passive form, or to put forth an action absolute, expressed by the neuter verb, or to assert its past, present, or future existence absolutely. . . . This personification of the subject of a proposition, which is still manifested in the forms and terminology of grammar, is an assimilation of things to an active, or at least demonstrative, self-consciousness or personality.[25]

Modern philosophers, Wright continued, see how misleading such syntax can be. They do not permit grammatical forms to mislead them into believing that physical objects are like conscious entities, exerting power to bring this or that about. But while the metaphysician is aware of the way syntax may mislead, he is unaware of the full extent of its power to mislead.[26] For what he himself retains in the form of substance is simply a refinement of the old notion that objects have power to manifest their properties. The metaphysician's refinement is this: physical substance is simply a matrix in which properties are embedded or glued together. He is not misled by syntax into thinking subject terms refer to personalized entities, but he is misled by the same structure of language into thinking they refer to depersonalized but still powerful entities, substrata or substances. According to Wright:

The subjects of propositions are still made to do the work, to bear the impositions, to make known the properties and accidents expressed by their predicates . . . just so far as they are supposed to be the names of anything but the assemblages of known essential qualities or phenomena actually coexistent in our experiences . . . or just so far as they are supposed to be the names of unknown and imperceptible entities.[27]

Wright finished this strand of his criticism of the concept substance by analyzing in detail Sir William Hamilton's view of it. One of his points is particularly interesting to us.

According to Wright, Hamilton believed in the existence of two metaphysical realities, mental and physical substances.[28] In the sentence "This pencil is round," "round" refers to an observable property of a physical substance designated in this case by the word pencil. In the sentence "I doubt," "doubt" refers to a psychological aspect (itself experienced) of a mental substance designated in this case by the word I. Hamilton also believed that while one could deny the existence of physical substance without paradoxical results, one could not deny the existence of mental substance without such results. After all, to doubt the existence of the subject would be to doubt the doubt, and thus neutralize it.

Wright was not impressed on this score with his old mentor. One can deny that a doubt inheres in a mental substance without denying the existence of the doubt as an experienced, psychological fact.[29] One justly ascribes a doubt to a self, but to a self composed of what it is experienced to be—an empirical self, not a metaphysical Self! Wright, in short, was just as eager to deny the existence of mental substance as physical substance. According to him, the reasons for believing in the former are the same as for believing in the latter—the misleading nature of syntax. The word I functions in its sentences in the same way as words like pencil function in theirs, and this function suggests the concept of mental substance just as a similar function of the word pencil suggests a physical substance.

Wright generalized his view about the misleading nature of syntax.[80] It explains not only the rise of concepts like mental and physical substance but also explains the rise of many other metaphysical notions, including the view that the concept of cause refers to an unobservable force in a cause which *makes* an effect occur. Wright observed, however, that to explain how such concepts arise is not to justify them. The nature of syntax is "sufficient to account for the existence of these beliefs and their cogency" but it does not give them any support.[81] Indeed, the point is just the opposite. If we see clearly how they arise from the misleading aspects of syntax, we should happily abandon these beliefs.

At this point Wright again brings into the picture certain biological views which nowadays seem irrelevant or at least unimportant.[82] If we ignore them, we see more clearly that Wright was anticipating the spirit of much contemporary philosophy when he talked about metaphysical notions arising from the misleading nature of syntax. If we do not ignore them, we are reminded again of the important point that a transition figure not only prefigures later events but is also rooted solidly in his own age.

Chapter 7

HISTORICAL BEARINGS

We have had occasional glimpses of Wright's importance in the history of American philosophy; but we need, finally, to set forth systematically his relation to other philosophers, before and after, both in America and England.

1. THE AMERICAN SCENE

Wright's life and thought must be viewed against the backdrop of nineteenth-century academic orthodoxy. He spent his whole life fighting the dogmatic view of philosophy advanced by people like James McCosh of Princeton and Andrew Preston Peabody of Harvard.

In the early part of the nineteenth century there was a resurgence of interest in Christianity.[1] There was a good deal of revivalism and emotional conversion. Denominations were formed and the churches began to wield more power. The colleges of America, usually denominational in nature, grew in strength and became strongholds of orthodox Christianity. The academic atmosphere became very pious indeed—among professors, at any rate, if not among students. The minister-philosophers of the colleges dispensed Christian thought to their students as *the* philosophy. The Socratic sense of philosophy as free

inquiry into any topic, however sacred, was simply
nonexistent. The academic orthodoxy had arisen
and was to flourish for the first three-quarters of the
century.

The philosophers who composed the academic
orthodoxy were legion; but the best known, perhaps,
were James McCosh of Princeton, Andrew Preston
Peabody of Harvard, Francis Bowen of Harvard,
Francis Wayland of Brown, Noah Porter of Yale,
James Fairchild of Oberlin, and Laurens P. Hickok
of Union. Also prominent, although not technical
philosophers, were Edward Hitchcock of Amherst,
Mark Hopkins of Williams, and Tayler Lewis of
New York University. In their books these men "il-
lustrated" philosophical truths, as they put it, rather
than drawing inferences from them.[2] The classroom
behavior of some of them points up their orthodoxy
even more dramatically. "The subjects [Wayland]
taught were presented as systems of immutable law
and of basic principle; student doubts were answered
by appeals to common sense, or to the conscience,
[or] occasionally by ridicule of the questioner."[3]
They were all equally pious and could be counted
on to select judiciously from scientific material those
facts which seemed most likely to bring science into
accord with Christianity. Their orthodoxy, moreover,
was quite independent of denominational lines. Unitarian Peabody was quite as academically orthodox
as Baptist Wayland.

Although belonging to different denominations, the
academic philosophers usually accepted the same
philosophical system as the basis of their orthodoxy
—namely, the Scottish common-sense views of
Thomas Reid and Dugald Stewart.[4] They accepted
Scottish philosophy not because it was dominated by

theology—it wasn't—but rather because it did not
conflict with anything in the various branches of
Protestantism and presented a highly acceptable conscience view of morality. After 1850 the influence
of German philosophy was increasingly felt, and the
academic philosophers lost their exclusively Scottish
bias and began to work the ideas of Kant and Hegel
into their defenses of orthodoxy.

As we have seen, Wright fought the Scottish and
Kantian views from first to last. After renouncing
his early allegiance to Hamilton, he devoted much
of his time to polemical writing against these foundations of America's academic orthodoxy. He argued
against the Scottish view that philosophical statements contradict common sense, and he claimed that
a priori knowledge in Kant's sense is impossible. He
argued in many other ways to show that only beliefs
based on experience count as knowledge. In all such
discussion he remained calm and unruffled. But his
battle against the academic philosophers in America
had a personal dimension. He wrote harshly sometimes because he felt that the dogmatism of the ministers endangered the very life and spirit of all philosophy. He was particularly bitter toward James
McCosh.[5] When McCosh wrote of a materialist that
his friends were praying for him "in all humility and
tenderness, that he and all others who had come under his influence may be kept from all evil," Wright
was thoroughly disgusted.

. . . to use the language of kindliness and mag-
nanimity when every page manifests an intense,
though smothered, *odium theologicum,* conceals
nothing, and repels more effectively than the most
open hostility. Expressions of petty spite, depre-

ciatory epithets, intimations of ill-opinion, readiness to credit evil reports of those who hold unorthodox opinions in philosophy, and misinterpretations of every sign of weakness in them—these characterize Dr. McCosh's treatment of those thinkers . . . who differ from him in fundamental views. If his object—supposing him to have an object in this—were simply to frighten the faithful from any contact with the unholy, we can see how he might effectively keep them faithful through ignorance; but if he thinks in this way to win anyone to his standard, we think he greatly mistakes the nature of the sceptic.[6]

Wright warred against the local Harvard orthodoxy—Peabody, Bowen, and Dr. Stearns of the Divinity School—just as lustily. These three men, he said, did more than anyone in Cambridge to keep the human mind in subjection.[7] He did not publish any polemical articles against their views primarily because he felt, no doubt, that their thought was not original enough to deserve it. But he fought them with his Socratic talk. In the late sixties and early seventies Wright attracted an increasing number of young Harvard graduates who, tired of the preaching at Harvard, sought him in his rooms for philosophical talk. He symbolized the rebirth of philosophy in the old Socratic sense of free inquiry into the foundations of knowledge instead of the orthodox ideal of finding reasons for beliefs already held. Sometimes Wright unintentionally made converts to his own specific views. Quite early his friend Charles Norton, son of the Unitarian theologian Andrews Norton, came to adopt his skeptical and agnostic views about religious questions. When Wright's name was later mentioned to the Reverend Grinnell of Charlestown, the reply was this: "He is, is he not, the one who led Charles Norton astray?"[8]

In 1869 Wright's skirmishes with the academic orthodoxy received unexpected reinforcement. In that year Charles William Eliot became President of Harvard, and in his inaugural address he said that "philosophical subjects should never be taught with authority."[9] One can well imagine Wright's look of satisfaction when Eliot went on to say:

> It is not the function of the teacher to settle philosophical and political controversies for the pupil. . . . The notion that education consists in the authoritative inculcation of what the teacher deems true may be logical and appropriate in a convent, or a seminary for priests; but it is intolerable in universities and public schools, from primary to professional.[10]

Wright's satisfaction must have been great indeed, for Andrew Preston Peabody—so long his intellectual foe—sat on the platform listening to it all. Peabody was in this unhappy position because he had been Interim President of Harvard. If he had become President instead of Eliot, academic orthodoxy would have remained secure at Harvard for many years to come. Henry James aptly remarked:

> If somebody like the Reverend Andrew Peabody had presided over Harvard during the seventies in place of young C. W. Eliot, and if D. C. Gilman had been made President of Yale instead of Noah Porter in 1871, the first American univer-

sity would have grown up in New Haven instead of in Cambridge.[11]

Unlike many college presidents, Eliot meant what he said in his inaugural address. He felt it was deplorable that old Professor Bowen should be the only source of instruction in philosophy, and "it was clear that the selection of other men to serve as correctives and antidotes and ultimately to replace him could not be guided by Bowen himself."[12] But Eliot was not content with supplementing and replacing Bowen in the philosophy department. He wanted philosophers of all opinions to be represented in the University Lectures, a kind of combined postgraduate and extension program. The first year these philosophers lectured: Emerson, Charles S. Peirce, F. H. Hedge, J. Elliott Cabot, G. P. Fisher, and John Fiske. Fiske's participation was the real key to Eliot's emancipated ideas, for only eight years before Fiske had been threatened with dismissal from college if he were caught talking Comtism to anybody![13] Even so, the real extent of the revolution was yet to be revealed. The next year Chauncey Wright was asked to participate in the lecture series, and he happily accepted this opportunity to carry his little campaign against Peabody and Bowen into the precincts of Harvard itself. One can visualize without much trouble the Reverend Grinnell of Charlestown sadly shaking his head over the decay of piety at Harvard.

While Wright was not successful as a teacher and was not asked to join the faculty permanently, his hope for better things at Harvard was not disappointed. In 1873 George Herbert Palmer, a really significant philosopher, was added to the philosophy department and such people as William James and Josiah Royce were soon to follow. What difference did it make who did the teaching as long as the goal of a university was achieved? In his essay on "The Conflict of Studies" Wright said that the whole point of a university is to encourage the pursuit of knowledge for its own sake. The point of a university is not to indoctrinate but to rectify the felt imperfections of knowledge. He quoted Mill approvingly: "If we were asked for what ends, above all others, endowed universities exist, or ought to exist, we should answer, 'To keep alive philosophy.' "[14]

2. THE LARGER SCENE

The view that Wright was a sophisticated follower of David Hume and John Stuart Mill seems to be the opinion of Wright's contemporaries. William James called Wright a worker on the path opened by Hume and observed that if he had written a treatise on psychology, it "would probably have been the last and the most accomplished utterance of what he liked to call the British School. He would have brought the work of Mill and Bain for the present to a conclusion."[15] John Fiske, another member of the Metaphysical Club, gave a similar interpretation. Could Wright have been induced to undertake an elaborate treatise, Fiske said, "we should have seen the philosophy of Mill and Bain carried to its highest development."[16]

There is, no doubt, a good deal of truth in these estimates of Wright. His similarity to Hume is clear in the following way. Wright believed that we should "try continually to test and correct our beliefs by the particulars of concrete experiences of a kind common to all." But this ideal, of course, is not always realizable. What of those religious beliefs for which an empirical test is conceivable but not available? Wright answered that one should hold such beliefs in a spirit which recognizes the absence of proof and so refrain from calling such belief knowledge. Questions which cannot *in principle* be empirically answered—like the question of whether anything exists when it is unperceived—are, Wright said, closed questions. While metaphysicians criticize empiricists for not answering such questions, the empiricist replies that these questions are idle and gratuitous and do not lead to a knowledge of anything.[17] Wright, in short, argued that only beliefs which yield, or could conceivably yield, to empirical evidence can count as knowledge. But this position is simply Hume's—stated so vividly in the chapter on skepticism in his *Enquiry Concerning Human Understanding:*

> If we take in our hand any volume; of divinity or school metaphysics, for instance; let us ask, *Does it contain any abstract reasoning concerning quantity or number?* No. *Does it contain any experimental reasoning concerning matter of fact and existence?* No. Commit it then to the flames: for it can contain nothing but sophistry and illusion.[18]

Wright also accepted Hume's analysis of causality, although he modified it in a way that we have already noted. If two events are causally related, then they must not simply be constantly but unconditionally conjoined. There must be no conceivable circumstances in which they could possibly break down.

Wright depended heavily on Mill in several ways. He accepted and defended Mill's brand of utilitarianism in every detail. He also got his notion of unconditional conjunction from Mill. In the beginning Wright also accepted Mill's phenomenalism. What one must mean by saying an object exists when unperceived, Mill said, and Wright agreed, is that *if* one were to go and look, one *would* receive certain perceptions. This permanent possibility of sensation constitutes the meaning of the expression "unperceived objects exist." In addition to agreeing with Mill on these general philosophical positions, he also followed Mill on certain details of psychology. For example, he distinguished two levels of rationality, according to whether associations by contiguity or similarity are operating.[19] Rote memorizing, he believed, is highly dependent upon associations by contiguity, while rational comprehension and invention depend upon associations of similarity. In this distinction Wright was following Mill, who had reintroduced association by similarity as a basic law of psychology after it had been banished by James Mill, who thought it was reducible to simple contiguity.[20]

There is another pervasive feature which Wright shared with nineteenth-century empiricists like Mill and Comte. Mill and Comte believed that scientific explanations may help directly in solving philosophical problems. Mill, for example, used the principles of associationistic psychology to show why only pleasure is experienced as intrinsically good. Comte, for his part, tried to show the meaninglessness of metaphysical concepts by giving an historical-sociological explanation of their occurrence. Wright, too, thought that scientific explanations help directly in solving philosophical problems. In his essay on "The

Evolution of Self-Consciousness," for example, he claimed that his psychological explanation of the origin of self-consciousness directly established the philosophical point that physical objects are neutral phenomena—the position later philosophers called neutral monism.[21]

In spite of his indebtedness to Hume, Mill, and the milieu of nineteenth-century empiricism, Wright was quite original in his thought and prefigured the spirit and content of much of modern philosophy. There were no models for his excellent studies in the philosophy of science that grew out of his criticism of Spencer and his defense of Darwin. Wright was a new kind of philosopher in the nineteenth century. He not only knew philosophy well but he was also technically proficient in mathematics, physics, botany and psychology. He published technical papers in these areas as well as in philosophy.[22] The fruits of the union of his philosophical and scientific knowledge were essays in the modern sense of philosophy of science—that is, the analysis of the logical structure and the basic concepts of the various sciences. There were few writers, before or since, more technically proficient for this new kind of work.

Wright, more than any other nineteenth-century empiricist, reoriented empiricism from concern over the origin of concepts and hypotheses to concern for their test or verification.[23] Empiricists tried hard to show that every concept and hypothesis was learned through experience, and they were pressed into odd explanations of how words like "infinite" could so arise. Wright insisted that the origin of a concept or hypothesis was irrelevant to the empiricist's position. Whatever the origin of concepts— whether through imagination, dreams, hallucinations or intuitions—the only important point is that the hypotheses in which they occur must yield consequences which can be checked or tested in experience. All empiricists nowadays accept this view of Wright's.

Wright was also forward-looking in his claim that philosophers do not contradict common sense in their philosophical assertions.[24] Common-sense knowledge must remain true in any philosophical analysis. Modern analytical philosophers, as we have seen, make precisely this same point.

Moreover, Wright did not stay long with Mill's concept of the permanent possibility of sensations. His notion of neutral phenomena was an important historical bridge between this phenomenalism and later concepts of neutral monism and sense-data theories. As we shall see in the next section, Wright passed the neutral notion along to William James and from him it went into the main stream of contemporary philosophy. Even in those cases where Wright drew most heavily on Mill's thought—namely, on the issues of morality and causality—he never failed to add an original touch and frequently defended utilitarianism more successfully than Mill. Finally, in his essay on self-consciousness he nicely supplemented Mill's associationistic psychology with the Darwinian concepts of minute variations and natural selection, thereby trying to account for the origin of rational behavior. Wright's pursuit of an empirical study of psychology marks him, along with other early psychologists, as a pioneer in the evolution of modern scientific psychology. In his *Principles of Psychology* James frequently drew on Wright's thought.[25]

The upshot of the discussion is that one ought not

to speak of Wright as a representative nineteenth-century philosopher. Further, it is misleading to speak of placing him in the main current of American philosophical thought. He helped much to change the main current of thought. He did not change it directly, to be sure, through teaching or writing, but through his influence on people like James, Charles S. Peirce, Oliver Wendell Holmes, Jr., and even John Dewey—all people who were far more successful than Wright in attracting the ear of the world.

3. WRIGHT'S INFLUENCE

Wright influenced no one in his two teaching ventures at Harvard. The class members either endured the ordeal or complained to the dean. Except for the English philosopher Samuel Alexander, he influenced no major thinker through his writing either. This fact is not surprising, for his essays make very difficult reading. According to John Fiske, "the difficulty—or, if we prefer so to call it, the esoteric character—of his writings was due . . . to the sheer extent of their richness and originality."[26] There are other reasons why Wright is not easily read. He never emphasized a point; everything in his essays, so to speak, is on a dead level. His work abounds in terse allusions which require enormous unraveling and interpreting. "Of such sort of obscure, though pregnant, allusions we have an instance in the use made of the conception of a 'spherical intelligence' in the essay on 'The Evolution of Self-Consciousness,' when the brief reference to the Platonic Timaios is by no means sufficient to relieve the strain

upon the reader's attention."[27] Finally, Wright rarely
gave concrete illustrations of the points he was making. (In *this* book the author often has supplied the
illustrations and examples of Wright's views.)

Wright's influence was felt primarily through philosophical discussion. Old friends like Norton, Gurney, Thayer, Abbot and Fiske, while not always
agreeing with him, quite often came around to his
way of thinking, or modified their own views in light
of what he had to say. And younger friends like
William James, Charles S. Peirce, and Oliver Wendell Holmes, Jr., acknowledged Wright to be their
intellectual boxing master during the early 1870's.[28]
Wright was the whetstone on which they sharpened
their philosophical wit. They learned a great deal
from him about the nature of philosophical analysis
—how to clarify, criticize, and compare. They
learned much about the nature of philosophical argument—how to check and parry an opponent's view
and organize and develop one's own. They got a
feel for the dialectical drift of philosophical argument. They were also influenced, both positively and
negatively, by Wright's own specific philosophical
views. James in particular was influenced in this way,
Peirce to a lesser extent.

Several recent commentators have written that
Peirce was led to formulate his pragmatic theory of
meaning through Wright's influence.[29] There may
have been some influence but we must be careful not
to exaggerate it. According to Peirce's pragmatic
theory of meaning, all empirical properties, however
simple, when predicated of an object, are hypotheses.
Thus, for example, "This diamond is hard" is a hypothesis which predicts that if I rub the diamond
across glass it will cut the glass, if I rub glass across

it the glass will not cut it, etc. The whole meaning of the sentence is the set of such possible sensory experiences. The meaning of any concept used in a sentence is simply the total of sensory consequences it entails if true.[30] Wright, however, never interpreted sentences like "This diamond is hard" as a hypothesis. For him only sentences which contain theoretical words—such as "This object is in uniform motion"—count as hypotheses. Nor did he ever say that the meaning of a sentence consists in its whole set of experienceable consequences; he only insisted that theoretical terms, to be admissible scientific notions, must have some sensory credentials, either by yielding sensory consequences themselves or by yielding such consequences in conjunction with other theoretical terms.

The disparity between Wright's and Peirce's thought is far greater than any similarity. Peirce called two of his fundamental concepts "tychism" and "synechism." His notion of tychism means that some events are uncaused, and his notion of synechism means that events show a developmental tendency toward greater regularity and uniformity.[31] Wright, as we have seen, heartily rejected both views; he insisted that every event has a cause and that physical events show on the whole no discernible tendency but rather exhibit the principle of countermovements.

Wright influenced James on a number of specific points, both positively and negatively. To see the different sorts of influence we must distinguish between the tender-minded and tough-minded sides of James's philosophy. To the former belong his book *The Varieties of Religious Experience* and his essay on "The Will to Believe." To the latter belong his books on *Pragmatism* and *Essays in Radical Empiricism*. In the tender-minded part of his philosophy James was in direct revolt against Wright's agnosticism and skepticism. In the early 1870's James was already arguing against his friend's agnosticism.[32] James argued that if one has insufficient evidence for either believing or disbelieving in God but nevertheless wants there to be a God, he has the duty to himself to believe as he wants. Wright was aghast! The only moral element in matters of belief, he said, is the obligation to carefully consider all available evidence. If one has done this but finds the evidence inconclusive, then he may choose to believe whatever he wants, but he has no duty one way or the other. James finally agreed with Wright's criticism.

Years later, after Wright was dead, James used his old friend's criticism for his own purposes in the "Will to Believe" essay. In this essay James was arguing against the agnosticism of William Kingdon Clifford, an English physicist. According to Clifford, if one has insufficient evidence, then it is his *duty* to suspend judgment, to be an agnostic. Not so, James countered. One has no duty either to believe or to disbelieve on insufficient evidence; having carefully considered the evidence, he is free to do either. James still thought of his old mentor when he wrote against agnosticism, for he mentioned Wright in a footnote in "The Will to Believe" essay. Moreover, there is some interesting unpublished material in the Harvard Houghton Library which suggests that James got one of the themes of this essay from reading Thayer's edition of Wright's *Letters*.[33] This theme was that inaction counts for action in the world of affairs and also in the religious world. If one is in-

CHAUNCEY WRIGHT

active like the agnostic, James said, and decides
nothing, he misses the chance of being on the right
side, if there is a God, just as much as the active
atheist who believes there is no God.

The tough-minded side of James' philosophy was
much influenced by his early association with Wright.
The most striking example of the influence in this
area is James' concept of pure experience, developed
in his *Essays on Radical Empiricism*.[34] James clearly
drew on Wright's concept of neutral phenomena.
James, like Wright, took great pains to deny the
existence of mental and physical substances. The
only reality of the world, he continued, is pure experience—that is, events unclassified into physical or
mental. Pure experience gets classified as physical
or mental through learning processes. Hence, James
concludes, the whole physical-mental classification is
a functional or practical one, not a metaphysical one.
James, in short, held a version of the neutral monist
position, and his version is similar at every point to
Wright's. Wright's term neutral phenomenon has one
advantage over James's term pure experience because
the latter, like Mill's concept of the permanent possibility of sensation, already suggests a sensory, perceptual or mental element. There are, to be sure,
minor differences between Wright and James on this
point. While Wright held that the physical-mental
distinction was a functional and not a metaphysical
one, he thought that any given individual always had
the capacity to make it. It is, Wright said, an instinctive response inherited from our ancestors.
James, however, insisted that each individual learns
the distinction through his own experience. There
are other differences, too, but they are matters of
further detail; there is complete agreement between

Wright and James on the main outlines of their neutral monism.

James was also influenced by Wright in his views on psychology. In his early essay on "Brute and Human Intellect," for example, James drew on Wright's distinction between sign-inference and reflective-inference to distinguish between animal and human intelligence.[35] There are many specific resemblances between James' discussion of reasoning in his *Principles of Psychology* and Wright's explanation of the origin of self-consciousness. James explicitly referred to Wright's work in a footnote in the chapter on reasoning.[36]

Wright's obvious influence on James's psychology takes on added interest when one realizes that Wright thereby may have had an eventual and indirect influence on John Dewey. In his article on "The Development of American Pragmatism," Dewey asserts that the instrumentalists (Dewey's name for his own version of pragmatism) found their genetic approach, their interpretation of thinking as an instrument for resolving problems, in James's *Principles of Psychology* rather than in his more philosophical books.[37] The source of the influence, according to Dewey, is contained particularly in James's chapters on Attention, Discrimination and Comparison, Conception, and Reasoning. Whatever influence, then, that Wright's genetic account of reasoning had on James himself increases in significance in its secondary and subsidiary influence, via James, on Dewey's views.

One must not, however, exaggerate similarities between Wright's and Dewey's thought. It is true that Wright's working-hypothesis interpretation of scientific principles and his denial that laws are summaries of observations is similar to Dewey's view. Dewey said that the pragmatists do not interpret general ideas simply as repeating and registering past experiences; rather they regard ideas as the bases for organizing future observations and experiences. According to Dewey, all ideas are working hypotheses, all thinking is experimental, scientific experimentation being only a limiting case of thinking in the sense of having ideal controls.

Wright certainly did not formulate a pragmatic view in anything like Dewey's general sense. All Wright did was to emphasize the instrumental, working-hypothesis nature of scientific concepts; he did not generalize this interpretation into an account of all thinking. If we say that Wright prefigured pragmatism, all we can mean is that he provided the logic of scientific inference which later philosophers *did* generalize into a pragmatic view of mind which holds all thinking to be instrumental. It is interesting to note, finally, that we have good evidence that Dewey had actually read Wright's *Philosophical Discussions*.[38]

It is clear that Wright influenced in subtle ways the thought of James, Peirce, and even Dewey. He also influenced Samuel Alexander and thinkers outside philosophy proper, like Oliver Wendell Holmes, Jr., St. John Green, and Henry Holland. Let it be granted that Wright was a seminal thinker, that many thinkers drew on his thought and writing, either knowingly or unconsciously. But we must not let a full appreciation of this fact obscure the even more important one of Wright's intrinsic merit. He has been too long unknown to the general philosophical reader. To be sure, he wrote rambling essays that are sometimes difficult to digest; but if one will take the time and trouble, he will discover an amazing richness, subtlety, and sophistication in his essays. His letters reveal, in addition to the portrait of a strong and original thinker, the figure of a man whose character is so different and so fine that it is difficult to describe in precisely the right way. His life was simple, and utterly devoid of any meanness. Fiske wrote that Wright "died as peacefully as he had lived,—on a summer's night, sitting at his desk with his papers before him. . . . To have known such a man is an experience one cannot forget or outlive."[39]

NOTES*

Chapter 1

1. Cf. E. W. Gurney's view of Wright's literary ability in James Bradley Thayer, ed., *Letters of Chauncey Wright,* pp. 377-78.

2. The sources for Wright's biography are his *Letters,* James Bradley Thayer, ed.; John Fiske, "Chauncey Wright" in *Darwinism and Other Essays;* William James, "Chauncey Wright" in *Collected Essays and Reviews;* and various unpublished material at Houghton Library, Harvard University, and at Duxbury, Massachusetts— specifically referred to in subsequent footnotes. Cf. also E. H. Madden, "The Cambridge Septem," and "Chauncey Wright's Life and Work: Some New Material."

3. Wright's *Letters,* James Bradley Thayer, ed., p. 30.

4. Cf. E. H. Madden's "The Cambridge Septem" for Thayer's records of this club.

5. Wright, letter to J. B. Thayer, May 24, 1865. Originally contained in the Duxbury material. I have turned this material over to the Houghton Library where it is being classified.

6. Susan Lesley, *Recollections of My Mother,* pp. 470 ff.

7. Norton reprinted all of these articles in Wright's *Philosophical Discussions.*

8. Cf. E. H. Madden, "George William Curtis: Practical Transcendentalist," *The Personalist,* Autumn, 1959, pp. 369-79.

* For bibliographical details, see the Annotated Bibliography.

NOTES

9. Cf. Philip P. Wiener's *Evolution and the Founders of Pragmatism*. Also cf. Wiener's reply to Herbert Schneider's review of his book in the *Journal of the History of Ideas*, XI (1950), No. 2.

10. William James, *Collected Essays and Reviews*, p. 20.

11. Houghton Library, Norton Collection, bMs Am 1088.1, 299. Cf. Wright's *Letters*, p. 159. Thayer deleted the names from the published letters.

12. Henry W. Holland in Wright's *Letters*, pp. 214-15.

13. Wright, *Letters*, p. 250.

14. *Ibid.*, p. 248.

15. *Ibid.*, p. 249.

16. William James, *Collected Essays and Reviews*, p. 25.

17. E. W. Gurney in Wright's *Letters*, pp. 382-83.

18. Cf. E. W. Gurney's intellectual portrait of Wright in Wright's *Letters*, pp. 361-83.

19. Cf. J. B. Thayer, *A Western Journey with Mr. Emerson* (Boston: Little, Brown, and Co., 1884), pp. 123-41.

20. E. W. Gurney in Wright's *Letters*, p. 365.

21. Sir William Hamilton, *Lectures on Metaphysics and Logic*, p. 101.

22. *Ibid.*, p. 100.

23. *Letters of Chauncey Wright*, p. 82.

24. Cf. Sir William Hamilton, *Discussions on Philosophy and Literature* (New York: Harper and Brothers, 1853), p. 156, n.

25. Cf. Charles Eliot Norton, *Letters*, ed. Sara Norton and M. A. De Wolfe Howe, Vol. I, p. 400.

26. Chauncey Wright, *Philosophical Discussions*, p. 426.

27. Cf. Simon Newcomb, "Abstract Science in America, 1776-1876." Newcomb felt that Gray and Wright were the most significant of all analysts on these philosophical aspects of Darwinism.

28. Cf. J. B. Thayer in Wright's *Letters,* p. 42, footnote 1.

29. Chauncey Wright, "The Faculties of Brutes," bMs Am 1088.5 (misc. 6), Box 11, The Norton Collection, Houghton Library, Harvard University.

30. E. W. Gurney in Wright's *Letters,* pp. 367-68.

31. Wright's "definition and defense" of Darwinism includes the following articles, all reprinted in *Philosophical Discussions:* "Limits of Natural Selection," "The Genesis of Species," "Evolution by Natural Selection," and "The Evolution of Self-Consciousness."

32. Wright, "The Philosophy of Herbert Spencer," reprinted in *Philosophical Discussions.*

33. Wright's *Letters,* p. 230.

34. Darwin in Wright's *Letters,* pp. 230-31.

Chapter 2

1. William R. Hutchison, *The Transcendentalist Ministers,* p. 4.

2. Cf. "Natural Theology As a Positive Science" in *Philosophical Discussions,* pp. 35-42.

3. *Ibid.*

4. *Ibid.,* pp. 39-40 ff.

5. *Ibid.,* pp. 40-41.

6. *Letters of Chauncey Wright,* p. 97.

7. Cf. Hutchison's excellent discussion of Andrews Norton in *The Transcendentalist Ministers.*

8. *Letters of Chauncey Wright,* p. 103.

9. Wright, *Philosophical Discussions,* pp. 357-59.

10. Wright quotes Mill in his *Philosophical Discussions,* pp. 357-58.

11. Cf. Wright, *Philosophical Discussions,* p. 358.

12. *Ibid.,* pp. 358-59.

13. *Ibid.,* p. 359.

14. Wright, *Letters,* pp. 133-34.

15. *Ibid.*, p. 133.

16. *Ibid.*, p. 285.

17. *Ibid.*, pp. 146-47.

18. *Ibid.*, p. 147.

19. *Ibid.*, pp. 114-19; pp. 141-42.

20. *Ibid.*, p. 115.

21. *Ibid.*, p. 114.

22. *Ibid.*, p. 118.

23. *Ibid.*, pp. 141-42.

24. Cf. Wright's "A Physical Theory of the Universe," reprinted in *Philosophical Discussions,* pp. 1-34.

25. Wright, *Philosophical Discussions,* p. 4. Wright said this of Aristotle but it applies equally well to himself.

26. Cf. E. H. Madden, *Chauncey Wright and the Foundations of Pragmatism,* Ch. 4, Section 3.

27. Wright, *Philosophical Discussions,* p. 9, text and footnote.

28. *Ibid.*, pp. 9 ff.

29. *Ibid.*, p. 87.

30. *Ibid.*

31. This theme runs through all of Wright's "A Physical Theory of the Universe." Cf. *Philosophical Discussions,* pp. 73-74.

32. *Ibid.*

33. *Philosophical Discussions,* pp. 17-34.

34. *Ibid.*, p. 10.

Chapter 3

1. Cf. E. H. Madden, *The Structure of Scientific Thought,* pp. 327-30.

2. Houghton Library, Norton Collection, bMs Am 1088.1, 250.

3. Wright, *Letters,* pp. 73-74.

4. Wright, *Philosophical Discussions*, pp. 131-32, p. 141.

5. Wright, *Letters*, p. 74.

6. *Ibid.*, pp. 74-75.

7. *Ibid.*

8. Cf. Wright, *Philosophical Discussions*, pp. 200-202, 378-82, 403-13. Later in the text we shall discuss this point in greater detail and in various contexts.

9. Wright's utilitarian views are to be found in his letters to Charles Eliot, Jane, and Grace Norton. See Index to Wright's *Letters*. The most important letters are reprinted from the original manuscripts in E. H. Madden, ed., *The Philosophical Writings of Chauncey Wright*.

10. Cf. Francis Wayland, *The Elements of Moral Science*, revised and improved edition, pp. 25-35.

11. Wright, *Letters*, p. 196.

12. Cf. Wayland, *Elements of Moral Science*, p. 39.

13. Wright, *Letters*, p. 196.

14. *Ibid.*, p. 197.

15. *Ibid.*, p. 290.

16. Cf. Wright, *Letters*, pp. 282, 291.

17. *Ibid.*, p. 291.

18. *Ibid.*, p. 282.

19. Cf. J. J. Chambliss, "Natural Selection and Utilitarian Ethics in Chauncey Wright" and E. H. Madden, *Chauncey Wright and the Foundations of Pragmatism*, Chapter 3, Section 4.

20. Charles S. Peirce, *Collected Papers*, Vol. V, paragraphs 12, 64.

21. Wright, *Letters*, pp. 114-18. Cf. particularly p. 117.

22. Cf. John Hospers, *Human Conduct* (New York: Harcourt, Brace and World, Inc., 1961), pp. 299-300. The example comes from E. F. Carritt's *Ethical and Political Thinking*, p. 64.

23. Wright, *Letters*, pp. 193-96.

24. *Ibid.*, p. 195.

25. *Ibid.*

26. *Ibid.,* pp. 195-97.

27. Francis Wayland, *Elements of Moral Science,* pp. 118 ff.

28. *Ibid.,* p. 122.

29. Cf. E. H. Madden, "George William Curtis: Practical Transcendentalist," *The Personalist,* Autumn, 1959, pp. 369-79; and Charles Robert Crowe, *George Ripley, Transcendentalist and Utopian Socialist* (Thesis, Brown University Library, 1955).

30. Cf. William Gordon Milne, *George William Curtis and the Genteel Tradition* (Thesis, Harvard College Archives, 1951), p. 35.

31. Cf. Crowe, *op. cit.,* pp. 133-34.

32. Wright, *Letters,* pp. 351-53.

33. *Ibid.,* p. 351.

34. *Ibid.,* pp. 351-52.

35. *Ibid.,* pp. 159-64.

36. *Ibid.,* pp. 160, 163.

37. *Ibid.,* p. 352.

38. *Ibid.,* p. 320.

Chapter 4

1. The most important essay in this vein is Wright's "The Philosophy of Herbert Spencer," reprinted in *Philosophical Discussions* and reprinted in part in *Philosophical Writings.*

2. Wright, *Philosophical Discussions,* p. 56. Wright's criticism of this view appears in numerous places in his "The Philosophy of Herbert Spencer." See pp. 43-96 in *Philosophical Discussions.*

3. Wright, *Philosophical Discussions,* p. 56.

4. *Ibid.,* p. 55.

5. *Ibid.,* pp. 46-47. This point is analyzed in more detail later in the text.

6. *Ibid.*, p. 76.

7. *Ibid.*, pp. 46-47.

8. *Ibid.*

9. This interpretation of Bacon has become the standard one. For a well-balanced discussion of Bacon's view see C. J. Ducasse's "Francis Bacon's Philosophy of Science" in *Theories of Scientific Method: The Renaissance Through the Nineteenth Century.*

10. Wright, *Philosophical Discussions*, p. 375. Cf. *ibid.*, pp. 376, 383, 400-405 for Bacon's real significance, according to Wright.

11. *Ibid.*, pp. 43-52. Cf. E. H. Madden, *The Structure of Scientific Thought*, pp. 13-19.

12. Cf. Philip P. Wiener's "Chauncey Wright's Defense of Darwin and the Neutrality of Science." Cf. Wright, *Letters*, p. 132.

13. Wright, *Philosophical Discussions*, p. 403. Cf. also, *ibid.*, pp. 376, 383, 400-405.

14. This theme permeates Wright's "A Physical Theory of the Universe" and "The Philosophy of Herbert Spencer."

15. Cf. particularly Wright's "The Philosophy of Herbert Spencer" and "The Genesis of Species."

16. Cf. Wright, *Letters*, p. 230.

17. Cf. Wright, *Philosophical Discussions*, pp. 168 ff. Also pp. 126-28.

18. *Ibid.*, pp. 137-38.

19. *Ibid.*, pp. 129-32.

20. *Ibid.*, pp. 131, 141.

21. *Ibid.*, p. 131.

22. *Ibid.*

23. G. J. Warnock, " 'Every Event Has a Cause,' " *Logic and Language, Second Series*, ed. A. G. N. Flew (Oxford: Basil Blackwell, 1953), p. 98.

24. Wright, *Philosophical Discussions*, pp. 183-86.

25. Wright added a short Appendix and the article was bound as a small book. It was entitled *Darwinism:*

Being an Examination of Mr. St. George Mivart's 'Genesis of Species', by Chauncey Wright, Esq. (London: John Murray, 1871). Copies of this volume are rare.

26. Philosophical Discussions, pp. 381-82.

27. G. H. Lewes, Problems of Life and Mind, II, iv, Section 49.

28. Wright, Philosophical Discussions, p. 201.

29. Ibid., pp. 199-200. Cf. ibid., pp. 200-202.

30. Cf. The Holmes-Laski Letters: The Correspondence of Mr. Justice Holmes and Harold J. Laski, 1916-1935, ed. Mark De Wolfe Howe (Cambridge: Harvard University Press, 1953), II, 1327-28.

31. C. S. Peirce, Collected Papers, Vol. VI, 28-45. One should read the whole of Peirce's essay on "The Doctrine of Necessity Examined." Cf. Vincent Tomas' Charles S. Peirce: Essays in the Philosophy of Science (New York: Liberal Arts Press, 1957), pp. 170-88. Note specifically p. 172.

32. Wright, Philosophical Discussions, pp. 200-201.

33. Ibid., pp. 375-84. Note specifically p. 379. Wright quotes McCosh.

34. Ibid., pp. 380, 381-82.

35. Ibid., p. 379. Wright quotes McCosh.

36. Ibid., pp. 379-82.

Chapter 5

1. Cf. Wright, "McCosh on Intuitions," reprinted in Philosophical Discussions, pp. 329-41.

2. Cf. E. H. Madden, "Chauncey Wright: Forgotten American Philosopher," particularly pp. 32-34.

3. Wright, Philosophical Discussions, p. 339.

4. Wright, Letters, p. 132.

5. Philosophical Discussions, p. 340.

6. Cf. E. H. Madden, "Chauncey Wright: Forgotten American Philosopher," particularly pp. 32-34.

7. For a short, clear exposition of Kant's concept of *a priori* knowledge, cf. Avrum Stroll and Richard H. Popkin, *Introduction to Philosophy* (New York: Holt, Rinehart & Winston, Inc., 1961), pp. 192-97.

8. *Ibid.*, p. 194.

9. Wright's most interesting discussion of *a priori* knowledge occurs in one of his letters to Francis E. Abbot. Cf. Wright's *Letters*, pp. 124-30. He criticized the notion of *a priori* knowledge in many of his reviews of Scottish philosophers. Cf. particularly his "McCosh on Intuitions," reprinted in *Philosophical Discussions*.

10. Wright, *Letters*, pp. 129-30; *Philosophical Discussions*, pp. 334-35.

11. Wright, *Letters*, p. 127.

12. *Ibid.*, p. 128.

13. *Ibid.*, p. 126.

14. *Ibid.*, p. 125.

15. For a clear exposition of Hume's analysis of the concept cause, cf. Stroll and Popkin, *Introduction to Philosophy*, pp. 113-19.

16. For criticisms of Hume's views see Stroll and Popkin, *op. cit.*, pp. 119-21.

17. *Philosophical Discussions*, pp. 245, 334-35.

18. *Ibid.*, p. 334.

19. William James, *The Principles of Psychology*, Vol. II, pp. 342-43.

20. Wright, *Philosophical Discussions*, pp. 245-48.

21. *Ibid.*, pp. 246-48.

22. *Philosophical Discussions*, pp. 348-49.

23. Cf. Sir William Hamilton, *Lectures on Metaphysics and Logic*, III, pp. 101, 102. Cf. II, p. 370.

24. Hamilton, *Lectures on Metaphysics and Logic*, III, p. 100.

25. Wright, *Philosophical Discussions*, p. 355.

26. *Ibid.*

27. Wright, *Letters*, p. 82.

28. Cf. Francis E. Abbot, "The Conditioned and the Unconditioned" and "The Philosophy of Space and Time."

29. Wright, *Letters,* pp. 61-62.

30. From E. H. Madden, *Chauncey Wright and the Foundations of Pragmatism,* Chapter 6, Section 1.

31. Cf. Wright, *Letters,* pp. 55, 76, 100, 108, 123, and 140.

32. *Ibid.,* p. 127.

33. *Ibid.,* pp. 76-80.

34. *Ibid.,* pp. 80, 82.

35. *Ibid.,* p. 82.

36. Wright, *Philosophical Discussions,* p. 249. Cf. *ibid.,* pp. 76, 367-68.

37. James makes this distinction in the first chapter of his *Pragmatism.*

Chapter 6

1. Wright, *Philosophical Discussions,* pp. 231-32.

2. Cf. Kurt Koffka, *Principles of Gestalt Psychology* (New York: Harcourt, Brace and Co., 1935), pp. 61 ff. Gestalt theory is not simply a psychological theory but also a full-blown philosophical position. Koffka and Wolfgang Köhler, another Gestalt theorist, are excellent examples of representative realists.

3. *Ibid.*

4. Cf. Avrum Stroll and Richard H. Popkin, *Introduction to Philosophy* (New York: Holt, Rinehart and Winston, Inc., 1961), pp. 99-113, 188, 189.

5. Cf. Wright, *Philosophical Discussions,* p. 348.

6. The philosopher nowadays makes this point by saying that the scientist works in an epistemologically constituted universe and hence what he does cannot solve philosophical problems.

7. Wright early followed J. S. Mill in interpreting physical objects as permanent possibilities of sensation, although he never discussed this notion in detail. Cf. *Letters*, pp. 131-32 and *Philosophical Discussions*, pp. 347-48.

8. David Masson, author of *Recent British Philosophy*, a book reviewed by Wright, argued in this way. Cf. *Philosophical Discussions*, pp. 347-48.

9. *Ibid.*

10. Wright's view of neutral phenomena is contained in his long essay on "The Evolution of Self-Consciousness," reprinted in *Philosophical Discussions*.

11. Cf. *Philosophical Discussions*, pp. 230-35.

12. *Ibid.*, pp. 205 ff.

13. *Ibid.*, p. 210.

14. *Ibid.*, p. 231.

15. *Ibid.*, p. 234.

16. Cf. John Hospers, *An Introduction to Philosophical Analysis* (New York: Prentice-Hall, Inc., 1953), pp. 413-20.

17. This point, of course, follows from Wright's general commitment to empiricism as well as from his specific commitment to neutral monism.

18. Cf. Hosper's discussion of sense-data theory in *An Introduction to Philosophical Analysis*.

19. Wright, *Letters*, p. 127.

20. Wright, *Philosophical Discussions*, p. 231.

21. *Ibid.*, pp. 237-38.

22. William James, "Chauncey Wright" in *Collected Essays and Reviews*, p. 24.

23. Wright, *Philosophical Discussions*, p. 235.

24. *Ibid.*

25. *Ibid.*, p. 236.

26. *Ibid.*, p. 237.

27. *Ibid.*

28. *Ibid.*, pp. 240-41.

29. *Ibid.*, p. 241.

30. *Ibid.*, pp. 238-39, 244 ff.
31. *Ibid.*, p. 239.
32. *Ibid.*, pp. 238-39.

Chapter 7

1. Cf. Joseph L. Blau, *Men and Movements in American Philosophy*, pp. 78-82.
2. *Ibid.*, p. 81.
3. Theodore Rawson Crane, *Francis Wayland and Brown University, 1796-1841*, 2, p. 542. (Ph. D. Thesis, Harvard University, 1959.) Cf. E. H. Madden, "Francis Wayland and the Limits of Moral Responsibility," *Proceedings of the American Philosophical Society*, CVI (1962), 348-49.
4. Blau, *op. cit.*, pp. 80-81.
5. Cf. Wright's "McCosh on Intuitions" and "McCosh on Tyndall," reprinted in *Philosophical Discussions*.
6. Wright, *Philosophical Discussions*, p. 377.
7. Houghton Library, Norton Collection, bMs Am 1088.1, 299. Cf. Wright's *Letters*, p. 159. Thayer deleted the names of Peabody, Bowen and the Cambridge Divinity School.
8. Houghton Library, Harvard University, Norton Collection bMs 1088, 8291.
9. Quoted by Henry James in his *Charles W. Eliot*, Vol. I, p. 231.
10. *Ibid.*
11. *Ibid.*, p. 224.
12. *Ibid.*, p. 253.
13. *Ibid.*, p. 250.
14. Wright, *Philosophical Discussions*, p. 283.
15. William James, *Collected Essays and Reviews*, p. 22.
16. John Fiske, *Darwinism and Other Essays*, p. 104.

17. Cf. Wright, *Letters,* p. 97, and *Philosophical Discussions,* pp. 348-49.

18. *Hume Selections* (New York: Charles Scribner's Sons, 1927), pp. 192-93.

19. Wright, *Philosophical Discussions,* pp. 291-92.

20. Cf. James Mill, *Analysis of the Phenomena of the Human Mind,* Vol. I, ed. J. S. Mill et al (London: Longmans, Green, Reader and Dyer, 1869), pp. 111 ff., text and footnotes.

21. *Philosophical Discussions,* pp. 230 ff.

22. Cf. Wright's *Letters,* pp. 41-42. As well as text, note footnote on p. 42.

23. *Philosophical Discussions,* pp. 46-47.

24. Cf. Wright's "McCosh on Intuitions," reprinted in *Philosophical Discussions.* Cf. also E. H. Madden, "Chauncey Wright: Forgotten American Philosopher," pp. 32-34.

25. Particularly in the chapter on Reasoning. James also acknowledged his indebtedness to Wright for intellectual comradeship in old times in the Preface to the *Principles of Psychology,* Vol. I, p. vii.

26. John Fiske, *Darwinism and Other Essays,* p. 81.

27. *Ibid.,* pp. 81-82.

28. Cf. William James, Preface to the *Principles of Psychology,* p. vii; and *The Collected Papers of C. S. Pierce,* Vol. 5, paragraph 12; Vol. 1, paragraph 4.

29. Morris R. Cohen, Introduction to C. S. Peirce's *Chance, Love, and Logic* (New York: Peter Smith, 1949), pp. xviii-xx. Cf. Gail Kennedy, "The Pragmatic Naturalism of Chauncey Wright," p. 498.

30. *Collected Papers of C. S. Peirce,* Vol. V, paragraph 9.

31. These themes recur throughout Peirce's *Collected Papers.*

32. Cf. Wright's *Letters,* pp. 341-43; and Ralph Barton Perry, *The Thought and Character of William James,* Vol. I, pp. 529-32. Thayer deleted James's name from Wright's *Letters.*

33. A note sent by James to Thayer, dated November 10, 1895. It was sent from 95 Irving Street, Cambridge. I have turned over this note to the Houghton Library, Harvard University, where it is now being classified.

34. Note particularly the first two essays.

35. Cf. Ralph Barton Perry, *Thought and Character of William James,* Vol. I, pp. 520 ff.

36. William James, *Principles of Psychology*, Vol. II, p. 359.

37. John Dewey, "The Development of American Pragmatism," *Studies in the History of Ideas,* Vol. II, ed. Department of Philosophy, Columbia University (New York: Columbia University Press, 1925), pp. 368-69.

38. John Dewey, "William James," *Journal of Philosophy,* VII, (1910), 505-506. Reprinted in Joseph Ratner, ed., *Characters and Events,* Vol. I (New York: Henry Holt and Co., 1929), pp. 107-08.

39. John Fiske, *Darwinism and Other Essays,* pp. 109-110.

ANNOTATED BIBLIOGRAPHY

1. Francis Ellingwood Abbot, "The Conditioned and the Unconditioned," *North American Review*, IC (1864), 402-48; and "The Philosophy of Space and Time," *North American Review*, IC (1864), 64-116. These articles contain Abbot's critique of Sir William Hamilton's view of space. Abbot asked Wright to comment on these two articles, and in his answering letters Wright worked out his own analysis of space and spatial relations.

2. ———, *The Syllogistic Philosophy* (Boston: Little, Brown and Co., 1906). The final statement of Abbot's "scientific theism." Josiah Royce referred to Abbot's philosophy as "warmed over" Hegelianism. Both Wright and Peirce, however, highly valued Abbot's work.

3. Paul R. Anderson and Max H. Fisch, *Philosophy in America* (New York: D. Appleton-Century Co., 1939). Reprints a long section of Wright's essay on "The Evolution of Self-Consciousness."

4. Joseph L. Blau, "Chauncey Wright: Radical Empiricist," *New England Quarterly*, XIX (1946), 495-517. An excellent analysis of Wright's moral philosophy.

5. ———, *Men and Movements in American Philosophy* (New York: Prentice-Hall, 1952). See Chapter 5, Section III, for an analysis of Wright's "positivistic psychozoology." Blau writes, "After the lapse of three quarters of a century, this dim figure emerges as one of the thinkers whose activity was central to the development of evolutionary naturalism in America," p. 168.

6. Catherine Drinker Bowen, *Yankee from Olympus:*

Justice Holmes and His Family (Boston: Little, Brown and Company, 1944). Note the references to Holmes' early associations with Wright. Wright always remained one of Holmes' favorite philosophers.

7. Francis Bowen, *Treatise on Logic: or, the Laws of Pure Thought: Comprising both the Aristotelic and Hamiltonian Analysis of Logical Terms* (Cambridge: Harvard University Press, 1865). For Wright's views on Bowen's work, see the *North American Review,* IC (1864), 592-605.

8. Borden Parker Bowne, "Chauncey Wright as a Philosopher," *New Englander,* XXXVII (1878), 585-603. A caustic criticism of Wright and empiricists in general from the standpoint of "personalistic idealism." Bowne, however, did appreciate Wright's critique of Spencer's philosophy.

9. J. J. Chambliss, "Natural Selection and Utilitarian Ethics in Chauncey Wright," *American Quarterly,* XII (1960), 144-59. Shows clearly and effectively how Darwin's notion of natural selection affected Wright's thinking in moral philosophy.

10. William Kingdon Clifford, *Lectures and Essays,* ed. Leslie Stephen and Sir F. Pollack, Vol. 2. (London and New York: The Macmillan Co., 1901). The most important essay in this volume, for our purposes, is "The Ethics of Belief." James was reacting against this piece in his "Will to Believe" essay—although, as a footnote about Wright in this essay suggests, it was the agnosticism of his old friend and mentor that still bothered him.

11. Morris R. Cohen, Introduction to Charles Sanders Peirce's *Chance, Love and Logic* (New York: Harcourt, Brace and Co., 1923). Cohen suggests that Peirce was led to formulate "the principle of pragmatism," a theory of meaning, through Wright's influence.

12. ———, "Later Philosophy" in *The Cambridge History of American Literature,* Part II, Vol. 3, ed. W. P. Trent et al, 226-65. (New York: G. P. Putnam's

Sons, 1921). Cohen suggests that Wright exerted a strong influence on William James's philosophy. Except for his reaction against Wright's agnosticism, James did take over a number of Wright's ideas, including the notion of "pure experience" which he discusses in his *Essays on Radical Empiricism*.

13. Charles Darwin, *Descent of Man* (New York: A. L. Burt, 1874). Darwin referred to Wright's essays in several places in this book. Cf. pp. 54, 651, 697.

14. ———, *The Origin of Species* (London: J. Murray, 1860). The most important intellectual influence in Wright's life. This epoch-making book not only thoroughly substantiated the fact of evolution but also offered the concept of natural selection as its explanation.

15. Francis Darwin, ed., *Life and Letters of Charles Darwin*, Vol. II (New York: D. Appleton and Co., 1888). The originals of Darwin's letters to Wright belong to descendants of Wright and are kept on file at the Alumni House, Smith College, Northampton, Massachusetts.

16. John Dewey, "The Development of American Pragmatism" in *Studies in the History of Ideas*, Vol. II, ed., Department of Philosophy, Columbia University (New York: Columbia University Press, 1925). A definitive view of the growth of American pragmatism.

17. ———, "William James," *Journal of Philosophy*, Sept. 15, 1910. Reprinted in Joseph Ratner, ed., *Characters and Events*, Vol. I, 107-08. (New York: Henry Holt and Co., 1929). In writing of James, Dewey said, "Classicists can doubtless explain how a man of such exquisite literary sense was the product of a scientific training. The student of his works notes both that his psychological career grew naturally out of his physiological interests, and that he was moved to strong reaction against the dogmatic attitude of many scientific men of that time. Chauncey Wright, I suppose, was one of the profoundest intellectual influences of his life—but in

the reverse direction [that is, away from dogmatism]."

18. Grace Edes, *Annals of the Harvard Class of 1852* (Cambridge: Harvard University Press, 1922). Contains interesting biographical information about Wright, Gurney, and Thayer, all of the Harvard Class of 1852. According to Edes, in 1884 some anonymous friend gave Harvard $500 for establishing the Chauncey Wright Fund, a scholarship for the encouragement of mathematics.

19. Ralph Waldo Emerson, *The Complete Works of Ralph Waldo Emerson*, Centenary Edition, 12 Vols. (Bostin: Houghton Mifflin Co., 1903-04). Note particularly Emerson's critique of historical Christianity in his "Divinity School Address." This piece influenced Wright considerably.

20. Max H. Fisch, ed., *Classic American Philosophers* (New York: Appleton-Century-Crofts, 1951). The important part of this book for our purposes is Fisch's "General Introduction." "One of the pioneers of our classical period, Chauncey Wright, early established himself as a leading philosophic interpreter and defender of the Darwinian theory," p. 12.

21. John Fiske, *Darwinism, and Other Essays* (London and New York: Macmillan and Co., 1879). Fiske's essay on Wright in this volume is appreciative and balanced.

22. ———, *Outlines of Cosmic Philosophy Based on the Doctrine of Evolutionism* (Boston: Houghton Mifflin Co., 1874). Wright believed that this work of Fiske's was far superior to that of Fiske's mentor, Herbert Spencer.

23. Sir William Hamilton, *Lectures on Metaphysics and Logic*, 4 vols., ed. H. L. Mansel and J. Veitch (Edinburgh: William Blackwood and Sons, 1882), Vol. III. These volumes, published after Hamilton's death, contain good material on the law of the conditioned and the nature of space—topics of great interest to Wright.

24. William Torrey Harris, *Hegel's Logic: A Book on*

the Genesis of the Categories of the Mind: A Critical Exposition (Chicago: S. C. Griggs and Co., 1890; second edition, 1895). Wright's opinion of Harris' philosophy was low. When Norton was editor of the *North American Review* he asked Wright's judgment of a paper Harris had submitted. Wright's judgment was so negative that Norton refused to publish it. By way of protest, Harris founded *The Journal of Speculative Philosophy*.

25. Richmond L. Hawkins, *Positivism in the United States (1853-1861)* (Cambridge: Harvard University Press, 1938). Hawkins' book helps one to see how little of a Comtist Wright was.

26. John Holmes, *Letters to J. R. Lowell and Others*, ed. W. R. Thayer (Boston: Houghton Mifflin Co., 1917). "I . . . sat up with Chauncey Wright (in the old house) till my illumination was exhausted, and we sat in darkness—[discussing] how he early developed a purpose of descending into the metaphysical abyss and how he disappeared as down a well, while I sat on the brink and listened to his still receding voice. . . ," p. 142.

27. Oliver Wendell Holmes, Jr., "The Holmes-Cohen Correspondence," *Journal of the History of Ideas*, Vol. 9 (1948). Holmes writes, "That we could not assert necessity of the order of the universe I learned to believe from Chauncey Wright long ago. I suspect C. S. P. got it from the same source," pp. 34 ff.

28. William R. Hutchison, *The Transcendentalist Ministers* (New Haven: Yale University Press, 1959). An excellent account of American unitarianism and the transcendental revolt against it. Unlike other accounts, this one does justice to the thought of the conservative unitarian Andrews Norton, the father of Wright's friend Charles Eliot Norton. For our purposes the best chapters are 1-4.

29. Henry James, *Charles William Eliot, President of Harvard University, 1869-1909* (Boston: Houghton Mifflin Co., 1930). The biographical parts are indispens-

able for understanding Eliot's major educational re-
forms. Cf. Chapters VII and VIII for a description of
the crucial years 1868-1878. Chapter VII contains an
excellent account of the educational system which was
dominant in Wright's day and against which, like Eliot,
he revolted.

30. William James, "Brute and Human Intellect,"
Journal of Speculative Philosophy, XII (1878), 236-76.
James is clearly influenced by Wright in this article
though he does not mention him by name. Cf. this
article with Wright's "Evolution of Self-Consciousness."

31. ———, *Collected Essays and Reviews* (New
York: Longmans, Green and Co., 1920). James refers
to Wright as "a worker on the path opened by Hume,"
p. 22. James felt that a long treatise by Wright would
have been the most accomplished utterance of British
empiricism.

32. ———, *Essays in Radical Empiricism* (New
York: Longmans, Green and Co., 1912). Here James
presents his concept of "pure experience." Cf. statements on pp. 14 and 23, particularly, with Wright's
essay on "The Evolution of Self-Consciousness."

33. ———, *Pragmatism* (New York: Longmans,
Green and Co., 1931). Some commentators feel that
James was influenced in the formulation of his "prin-
ciple of pragmatism" by Wright's emphasis on the
working-hypothesis nature of scientific hypotheses. Cf.
James' formulation of the principle on pp. 46-47 with
Wright's essay on "The Philosophy of Herbert Spencer."
Cf. also E. H. Madden's *Chauncey Wright and the
Foundations of Pragmatism*, Ch. 4, Section 2.

34. ———, *Principles of Psychology*, 2 vols. (New
York: Henry Holt and Co., 1896). Concerning the ev-
olution of self-consciousness, James explicitly draws on
Wright's work, as he indicates in a footnote on p. 359,
Vol. II.

35. ———, *The Will to Believe and Other Essays on*

Popular Philosophy (New York: Dover Publications, Inc., 1956). Although James explicitly criticizes the agnosticism of William Kingdon Clifford, he still had his old friend Wright in mind when he wrote his "Will to Believe" essay. Cf. E. H. Madden, *Chauncey Wright and the Foundations of Pragmatism*, Ch. 2, Section 3.

36. ————, unpublished note to James Bradley Thayer; Houghton Library, William James Letters, bMs Am. 1092.1. Suggests that Wright got a central idea of his "Will to Believe" essay—namely, that inaction sometimes counts for action—from a comment by Thayer in Wright's *Letters*. Cf. E. H. Madden, *Chauncey Wright and the Foundations of Pragmatism*, Ch. 2, Section 3.

37. Gail Kennedy, "The Pragmatic Naturalism of Chauncey Wright," in *Studies in the History of Ideas*, Vol. III, ed. Department of Philosophy, Columbia University. (New York: Columbia University Press, 1935). A pioneer study of Wright's philosophy; Kennedy conceives Wright to be in some ways a precursor of pragmatism.

38. Susan Lesley, *Recollections of My Mother* (Boston: Houghton Mifflin Co., 1875). Mrs. Lesley wrote appreciatively of Wright's helpfulness to her mother, Mrs. Lyman. She felt he boarded at Mrs. Lyman's in order to give support and steadiness to the lonely woman. Cf. pp. 470 ff.

39. A. O. Lovejoy, "The Thirteen Pragmatisms," *Journal of Philosophy*, V (1908), 5-12. Shows the ambiguity of the doctrine of pragmatism. Lovejoy was convinced that one could discover even more than thirteen meanings of the word if he searched diligently enough. This ambiguity suggests that one must guard carefully any statements about Wright's prefigurement of "pragmatism."

40. Edward H. Madden, "The Cambridge Septem," *Harvard Alumni Bulletin*, LVII (1955) 310-15. Thayer's records of the meetings of the Septem. It is a vignette

of young life in old Cambridge and makes light and entertaining reading.

41. ———, "Chance and Counterfacts in Wright and Peirce," *The Review of Metaphysics*, IX (1956), 420-32. An analysis of Wright's concepts of "cosmic weather," "accidents," and "irregularity." An effort to show that Wright in no way prefigured Peirce's "tychism."

42. ———, "Chauncey Wright: Forgotten American Philosopher," *American Quarterly*, IV (1952), 24-34. A general survey of Wright's philosophy. Notice particularly the section on Wright's views of common-sense knowledge.

43. ———, *Chauncey Wright and the Foundations of Pragmatism* (Seattle: University of Washington Press, 1963). An extended analysis of Wright's life and thought and his intellectual influence on Pierce, James and a host of other philosophers.

44. ———, "Chauncey Wright's Life and Work: Some New Material," *Journal of the History of Ideas*, XV (1954), 445-55. Based on hitherto unpublished manuscripts in the Houghton Library, Harvard University, and on manuscripts in the possession of Mrs. Frances Ames Randall, Duxbury, Massachusetts. Much of this material has now been given to the Houghton Library. This article also reprints Wright's college theme entitled "Whether the faculties of Brutes differ from those of men in kind or in degree only?"

45. ———, ed., *The Philosophical Writings of Chauncey Wright: Representative Selections* (New York: The Liberal Arts Press, 1958). The most important and most readable of Wright's essays and letters. The selections are reprinted from the original essays in the *North American Review* and the *Nation* and from the original letters in the Houghton Library. This procedure was necessary since Norton and Thayer edited the *Philosophical Discussions* and the *Letters* with unnecessary prudence.

46. ———, "Pragmatism, Positivism, and Chauncey

Wright," *Philosophy and Phenomenological Research,*
XIV (1953), 62-71. Contains the claim that Wright
prefigured pragmatic "theories" of mind, meaning, and
truth only in very attenuated ways. An effort is made to
point up Wright's intrinsic significance.

47. ———, *The Structure of Scientific Thought* (Boston: Houghton Mifflin Co., 1960), pp. 13-19. Reprints
a section of Wright's essay on "The Philosophy of
Herbert Spencer." It contains Wright's explanation of
the rapid rise of modern science.

48. ———, "Wright, James, and Radical Empiricism," *Journal of Philosophy,* LI (1954), 868-74. Shows
the ways in which Wright influenced James in his concept of "pure experience," found in *Essays on Radical
Empiricism* and in his chapter on reasoning in *The
Principles of Psychology.*

49. ———, ed., with R. M. Blake and C. J. Ducasse,
*Theories of Scientific Method: The Renaissance through
the Nineteenth Century* (Seattle: University of Washington Press, 1960), Chapters 12 and 13. Chapter 13
deals with Wright's views that "every event has a cause"
and that science is metaphysically neutral, and with the
implications of his thought for the logic of psychological explanation.

50. ——— and Marian C. Madden, "Chauncey
Wright and the Logic of Psychology," *Philosophy of
Science,* XIX (1952), 325-32. Relates Wright's psychological views to traditional British associationism and to
the later functional psychology of James, J. R. Angell,
and John Dewey.

51. James McCosh, *The Scottish Philosophy: Biographical, Expository, Critical, from Hutcheson to Hamilton* (New York: R. Carter and Bros., 1875). Wright
considered McCosh to be the worst of the "presumptuous orthodoxy." Cf. Wright's review of McCosh in the
Nation, I, No. 20, 627.

52. John Stuart Mill, *Examination of Sir William
Hamilton's Philosophy,* 6th ed. (London: Longmans,

Green, and Co., 1889). In Wright's view this book greatly diminished Hamilton's philosophical reputation. Note particularly Mill's criticism of Hamilton's view on space.

53. ———, *A System of Logic* (London: Longmans, Green and Co., 1895). Wright considered Book III, "Of Induction," the most valuable part of this work. Cf. Book III, Ch. VI, "Of the Composition of Causes," with Wright's discussion of the two types of explanation in his criticism of McCosh.

54. ———, *Utilitarianism* (Boston: W. Small, 1887). In his "Commemorative Notice" of Mill, Wright said, "He redeemed the word 'utility' from the ill repute into which it had fallen, and connected noble conceptions and motives with its philosophical meaning." Cf. E. H. Madden, *The Philosophical Writings of Chauncey Wright*, p. 122.

55. St. George Mivart, *On the Genesis of Species* (London: Macmillan and Co., 1871). Mivart here accepts the fact of evolution but rejects Darwin's explanation of it by the notion of natural selection. Wright criticizes this book in his article "The Genesis of Species," which appeared in the *North American Review*, July, 1871.

56. ———, letter to Editor of *North American Review*, April (1872). Mivart's answer to Wright's criticism. Wright replied to this letter in his article on "Evolution by Natural Selection," *North American Review*, July, 1872.

57. Simon Newcomb, "Abstract Science in America, 1776-1876," *North American Review*, Vol. CXXII (1876). ". . . In philosophic comprehension, scientific accuracy, and clearness of thought, the essays of Wright and of Gray might well head the list in a competition among those of all nations," p. 109.

58. Charles Eliot Norton, ed., *Chauncey Wright's Philosophical Discussions* (New York: Henry Holt and Co., 1877). A collection of Wright's essays and reviews.

Norton's "Introduction" to this book is excellent. Unfortunately, he edited too freely, sometimes deleting without any indication that anything of the original article was left out.

59. ———, letters to Wright (Siena, June 12, 1870; September 13, 1870). Houghton Library, Norton Collection, bMs Am. 1088.2. Contains Norton's view on utilitarianism and its relation to aesthetic values. These letters prompted Wright to work out his own moral views. Superficial excerpts from these letters appear in *Letters of Charles Eliot Norton.* Cf. Vol. I, pp. 385 and 398. Cf. also E. H. Madden, "Charles Eliot Norton on Art and Morals," *Journal of the History of Ideas,* XVIII (1957), 432-33.

60. Sara Norton and M. A. De Wolfe Howe, eds., *Letters of Charles Eliot Norton,* 2 vols. (Boston: Houghton Mifflin Co., 1913). The editors underplay Norton's agnosticism and skepticism and Wright's influence on him. Norton's letters are rich sources for students of American literary and art history.

61. George Herbert Palmer, *The Problem of Freedom* (Boston: Houghton Mifflin Co., 1911). Palmer became assistant professor of philosophy at Harvard in 1873. He was influenced partly by Wright to reject the indeterminist position on the problem of freedom and moral responsibility.

62. Charles Sanders Peirce, *Collected Papers,* ed. Charles Hartshorne, Paul Weiss, and Arthur Burks (Cambridge: Harvard University Press, 1931-58). All of Peirce's important works are now available in this series. For Peirce's version of the pragmatic principle, cf. Vol. 5, paragraphs 403, 411, and 412. Cf. E. H. Madden, "Pragmatism, Positivism, and Chauncey Wright," *Philosophy and Phenomenological Research,* XIV (1953), particularly Section II.

63. Ralph Barton Perry, *Annotated Bibliography of the Writings of William James* (New York: Longmans, Green and Co., 1920). Perry suggests that Wright ex-

erted a strong positive influence on James's thought (excepting, of course, Wright's agnosticism).

64. ———, *The Thought and Character of William James*, Vol. I. (Boston: Little, Brown, and Company, 1935). The definitive study of James's life and thought. Perry publishes Wright's letter to Grace Norton, dated July 18, 1875, in which he said of James, "He rather attracts me by the Jamesian traits; crude and extravagant as are many of his opinions, and more especially his language." Cf. pp. 530-32.

65. Noah Porter, *The Human Intellect: with an Introduction upon Psychology and the Soul* (New York: Charles Scribner's Sons, 1868). Porter's discussion of the problem of perception shows marked similarity to the thoughts of Thomas Reid and Sir William Hamilton. Porter, along with Wayland and Hickok, is a good representative of the "academic orthodoxy" which Wright fought so vigorously.

66. Sidney Ratner, "Evolution and the Rise of the Scientific Spirit in America," *Philosophy of Science*, Vol. III (1936), pp. 104-22. Contains the unsupported claim that Wright *founded* the pragmatic movement.

67. Herbert W. Schneider, *A History of American Philosophy* (New York: Columbia University Press, 1946). Numerous and scattered references to Wright. "Unfortunately, Wright died soon after he had formulated [a new radical empiricism], and no one can tell whether if he had lived longer he would have developed it in the direction of Peirce or of James," p. 521. Cf. E. H. Madden, "Wright, James, and Radical Empiricism," pp. 868-74.

68. Herbert Spencer, *Works* (New York and London: D. Appleton and Co., 1910). A highly influential philosophy, particularly in America. Even farmers and mechanics had their copies of Spencer's works. Jack London also found them to be his philosophical favorites. To Wright, however, Spencer was an intellectual

cadaver, the dissection of which helped sharpen philosophical perception.

69. James Bradley Thayer, ed., *Letters of Chauncey Wright* (Cambridge: John Wilson and Son, 1878). Thayer's biographical account is interesting and well written. However, he edited Wright's letters too prudently, deleting names from sentences that might offend, and he wildly altered without comment Wright's punctuation and sentence structure. Cf. the letters to Charles, Grace, and Jane Norton in *The Letters* with the originals in the Houghton Library.

70. ———, unpublished letter to C. E. Norton, Houghton Library, Norton Collection No. 7325. This letter is dated September 16, 1877. Thayer is writing to Norton about his preparation of Wright's *Letters*. ". . . There were several difficult points—especially how to deal with the one sad fact of Chauncey's life. . . . I have received information, which troubled me, within a week or two as to the beginning of dangerous habits as early as 1862 and I had to rewrite some things in the light of it. Nichols tells me that he and Wyman both, *at the time,* attributed Chauncey's difficulty in 1863 to the effect of too much alcohol, and this is unfortunately fortified by some other facts. But there is nothing to indicate excess then in the sense of what came in 1868 or so."

71. ———, unpublished material found at Duxbury, Massachusetts. Includes note of William James to Thayer (Nov. 10, 1895); three letters from Wright to Thayer; a letter from Wright to Miss Robbins (August 7, 1864); letter from Mrs. Lesley to Thayer about Wright's funeral; and numerous other letters and memoranda. I have turned over most of this material to Houghton Library.

72. Alfred Russel Wallace, *Contributions to the Theory of Natural Selection* (London: Macmillan Co., 1870). Wallace restricted the concept of natural selection to the development of lower animals and to

the physical development of man, but he denied that it could be applied properly to the evolution of man's mental and moral character. Wright criticized Wallace's position in his essay on the "Limits of Natural Selection," *North American Review*, October, 1870.

73. Francis Wayland, *The Elements of Moral Science* (Boston: Gould, Kendall and Lincoln, 1873). (First edition, Boston: Gould, Kendall and Lincoln, 1835.) A clear, concise, and interesting presentation of the conscience theory of morality which Wright constantly opposed. This book sold 200,000 copies in the sixty years it was marketed. Note particularly the chapter on natural theology where Wayland incorporates utilitarian principles into his own moral system.

74. Philip P. Wiener, "Chauncey Wright's Defense of Darwin and the Neutrality of Science," *Journal of the History of Ideas*, VI (1945), 19-45.

75. ———, *Evolution and the Founders of Pragmatism* (Cambridge: Harvard University Press, 1949). In this article and book, Wiener cogently claims that one of Wright's central contributions to philosophy is showing the metaphysical neutrality of scientific investigation.

76. Chauncey Wright, "The Faculties of Brutes," Harvard College Library, The Norton Collection, bMs Am 1088.5 (misc. 6), Box 11. The forensic paper of Wright's in which he argued, against his teacher Dr. Walker, that the faculties of brutes differ from man's in degree only and not in kind.

77. ———, Letter to Ralph Waldo Emerson (1865), Houghton Library, bMs Am. 1280 (3554). Written in his capacity as Secretary of the American Academy of Arts and Sciences.

78. ———, *Letters*, ed. James Bradley Thayer (Cambridge: John Wilson and Son, 1878). Thayer's biographical account is interesting and well written. However, he edited the *Letters* too prudently, deleting names from sentences that might offend, and he wildly

altered without comment Wright's punctuation and sentence structure.

79. ———, "Letters to Charles Eliot Norton, Grace Norton, and Jane Norton," (Harvard College, Houghton Manuscript Library, bMs Am. 1088, 1088.1). Cf. these original letters with Thayer's version in the *Letters*. These letters contain most of Wright's moral philosophy.

80. ———, *Philosophical Discussions*, ed. C. E. Norton (New York: Henry Holt and Co., 1877). A collection of Wright's essays and reviews. Norton's "Introduction" to this book is excellent. Unfortunately, he edited too freely, sometimes deleting without any indication that anything of the original article was left out.

81. ———, *Philosophical Writings: Representative Selections*, ed. Edward H. Madden (New York: Liberal Arts Press, 1958). The most important and most readable of Wright's essays and letters. The selections are reprinted from the original essays in the *North American Review* and the *Nation* and from the original letters in Houghton Library.

82. ———, short articles and reviews, not reprinted in any book. In the *Nation:* "Mill on Hamilton," I, No. 9, 278; "Mill on Comte," II, No. 27, 20; "Spencer's Biology," II, No. 55, 724; "Martineau's Essays," II, No. 60, 804; "Ennis on the Origin of Stars," IV, No. 90, 231; "The Reign of Law," IV, No. 102, 470; "Note to 'Mathematics in Court,'" V, No. 116, 238; and "Bledsoe's 'Philosophy of Mathematics,'" VI, No. 148, 355. In the *North American Review:* "Chauvenet's Manual of Astronomy," Vol. IIC (1863), 611; "Bowen's Logic," IC (1864), 592-605; "Correlation and Conservation of Forces," C (1865), 619-22; "American Ephemeris and Nautical Almanac," CI (1865), 134 ff.; "Draper's Future Civil Policy of America," CI (1865), 589; "The Right of Suffrage," CIII (1866), 241-250; "Mill on Hamilton," CIII (1866), 250-260; "Alden's Philosophy," CIII (1866), 260-269; "Spare's Differen-

tial Calculus," CIII (1866), 308 ff.; "Ennis' Origin of the Stars," CIV (1867), 618 ff.; "Chapin on Gravity and Heat," CV (1867), 330 ff.; "Peabody's Positive Philosophy," CVI (1868), 285 ff.

INDEX

a priori knowledge, 82-85
Abbot, Francis E., 6, 90, **93**
Agassiz, J. L. R., 17, 71
Agnostics, 33
Alexander, Samuel, 74, **75**, 126, 132
Archimedes, 65
Aristotle, 66, 67
Astronomy, 80

Bacon, Francis, 3, 64, 66
Bain, Alexander, 15, 121
Bentham, Jeremy, 50
Bergson, Henri, 74
Bowen, Francis, 7, 116, 118, 120
"Brute and Human Intellect" (James), 131

Cabot, J. Elliott, 120
Calvinists, 32
Carnap, Rudolf, 63
Causality, 39-43, 125
  concept of, 70-71, 86-89, 122
Chambers, Robert, 2, 17, 18
Christianity, 24-27, 33
  American Colleges and, 115-116
  Philosophy and, 115-116, 117
Clifford, William Kingdon, 129
Colleges, American, 115
Comte, Auguste, 33, 123

"Conflict of Studies, The" (Wright), 121
Cosmology, Non-Theistic, 33-38
Curtis, George W., 5, **53-54**
Cuvier, Baron, 18

Darwin, Charles Robert, 1, 3, 12, 16-17, 18, 59, 124
  natural selection and, 22, 48, 67-72
Darwin, Charles Robert (Mrs.), 10
Darwin, Horace, 10
Determinism, 40-44, **75-76**, 78
"Development of American Pragmatism, The" (Dewey), 131
Dewey, John, 126, **131-132**
Dogmatists, 66

Eliot, Charles William, 6, 7, 120
  quoted, 119
Ellis, Reverend, 29
Emergence, doctrine of, 74-75
Emerson, Ralph Waldo, **3**, 53, 54, 120
  morality and, 12
Emotions and the Will, The (Bain), 15
Empiricism, 33, 66, 84, 109-110, 122, 124-125

[165]

Enquiry Concerning Human Understanding (Hume), 122

Essay on Liberty (Mill), 16

Essays in Radical Empiricism (James), 129, 130

Evolution, 67
solar system and, 34-38
See also Natural Selection; Science, Darwinian

"Evolution by Natural Selection" (Wright), 67

"Evolution of Self-Consciousness, The" (Wright), 79, 97, 104, 109, 123-124, 126

Examination of Sir William Hamilton's Philosophy (Mill), 16

Fisher, G. P., 120

Fiske, John, 6, 18, 120, 121, 126, 127

Galileo, 60, 65, 66-67

Genesis of Species (Mivart), 18

"Genesis of Species, The" (Wright), 19, 67, 72

Geometry, 83-84

Gilman, D. C., 119

Gray, Asa, 17, 22

Green, Nicholas St. John, 6, 132

Grinnell, Reverend, 119, 120

Gurney, E. W., 3, 4, 5, 7-8
quoted on C. Wright, 11

Hallucinations, 98-99, 105, 106-107, 124-125

Hamilton, William (Sir), 3, 12, 117
"Law of the Conditioned" and, 91-92, 93

John Stuart Mill and, 16, 93
theories on space, 13-14, 90-92, 93-94, 95

Harvard College, 1, 2-3, 6, 7, 118-119, 120

Hedge, F. H., 120

Hegel, Georg W. F., 117

Hickok, Laurens P., 116

Hitchcock, Edward, 116

Holland, Henry W., 132
quoted on C. Wright, 7

Holmes, Oliver Wendell (Jr.), 6, 8, 126, 127, 132

Hopkins, Mark, 116

Hume, David, 15, 62, 86, 87, 88, 89, 100, 121-122, 124

Illusions, 98-99, 105-106

In Memoriam (Tennyson), 27-28

Indeterminism, 40-41

James, Henry (Jr.), 10

James, Henry (Sr.), 10

James, William, 8
agnosticism and, 128-131
doctrine of pure experience, 108, 130
Harvard College and, 121
David Hume and, 88
physical-mental classification of, 130
quoted, 5, 110
Chauncey Wright and, 96, 125, 126, 127, 132

Kant, Immanuel, 81-85, 117

Language, syntax and, 112-114

Laplace, Pierre S., 37

"Law of the Conditioned" (Hamilton), 91-92

Laws, ultimate, 89
Lectures on Metaphysics and Logic (Hamilton), 13
Lehrbuch auf Botanik (journal), 16
Lesley, Mary, 4, 58
Lesley, Susan, 4, 58
Letters (Wright), 1, 56, 57, 129-130
Lewis, Tayler, 116
"Limits of Natural Selection, The" (Wright), 67
Logicians, 71-72
Lowell, Charles (Mrs.), 3
Lyman, Ann, 2, 4

McCosh, James, 76-77, 79, 115, 116, 118
Mansel, H. L., 26
Materialism, 76-78
Memorizing, rote, 123
Metaphysical Club, 6
Metaphysics, 65-66, 89, 90-92, 95, 96, 109, 110, 111-114, 122
Mill, John Stuart, 3, 12, 124
　characteristics of, 33
　empirical philosophy of, 62
　on good and evil, 25-26
　Hamilton's philosophy and, 16, 93
　pleasure and, 50-51
　quoted, 121
　scientific explanation and, 123
　utilitarianism of, 15-16, 47
　views adapted by Wright, 102, 125
Miracles, 24
Mivart, St. George, 18-19, 69
Morality, 58
　causality and, 39-43, 125
　determinism, 40-44
　human behavior and, 39-41
　indeterminism, 40-41
　moral responsibility, 39-40, 42-43, 129
　reason and, 43-44
　reform and, 53-57
　religion and, 26-27, 31
　utilitarianism, 44-53
Morgan, Lloyd, 74

Nation, 1, 5, 9
Natural Selection, 22
　concept of, 68-70, 125
　Charles Darwin and, 22, 48, 67-72
　evolution of species in, 68, 71-72
"Natural Theology as a Positive Science" (Wright), 23
Nautical Almanac, 1, 3
Nebular hypothesis, 36-37
Neutral monism *see* Neutral phenomena
Neutral phenomena, 103-104, 105, 108, 124-125, 130
Newcomb, Simon, 42
Noncontradiction, law of, 92
North American Review, 1, 5, 18, 23, 67
Norton, Andrews, 24, 118
Norton, Charles Eliot, 1, 5, 11, 16, 32-33, 118, 127
Norton, Charles Eliot (Mrs.), 5
Norton, Susan *see* Norton, Charles Eliot (Mrs.)

Objects, physical, 109-114, 122-123
　common-sense view of, 97-98, 99, 101, 125
　hallucinations, 98-99, 105, 106-107, 124-125

Objects, Physical (*cont.*)
  illusions, 98-99, 105-106
  Neutral phenomena, 103-
    104, 105, 108, 124-
    125, 130
  phenomenalism, 102-103,
    123, 125
  realism and, 99-101, 104,
    105
  sensation and, 99-101, 102,
    125, 130
  Sense-data, 105, 107, 109,
    125
  subjective idealism and,
    101-102, 104, 105
Origin of Species (Darwin),
    16-17

Palmer, George Herbert,
    120-121
Parker, Theodore, 53-54
Peabody, Andrew, 7, 115,
    116, 118, 119, 120
Peirce, Benjamin, 2
Peirce, Charles S., 6, 8, 48,
    75-76, 20, 126, 127, 132
Phenomenalism, 102-103,
    123, 125
Philosophical Discussions
    (Wright), 1, 75, 132
"Philosophical optimism"
    see Ultimate harmony
    view
Philosophy, 3
  American school of, 115-
    121, 126
  British school of, 121-122
  Christianity and, 115-116,
    117
  German, 117
  William Hamilton and, 3,
    12, 13-14, 16, 90-92,
    93-94, 95, 117
  Harvard College and, 118-
    119, 120
  Kantian, 117

John Stuart Mill and, 3,
    12, 15-16, 33, 47,
    50-51, 62, 93, 102,
    123, 124, 125
  Scottish school of, 79-80,
    116-117
"Philosophy of Herbert
    Spencer, The" (Wright),
    36
*Philosophy of the Uncondi-
    tioned* (Hamilton), 13
Porter, Noah, 116, 119
Pragmatism, 131-132
Pragmatism (James), 129
Principles of Psychology
    (James), 125, 131
Protestantism, morality and,
    117
Psychology, associationistic,
    123, 125
Ptolemy, 65

Reid, Thomas, 79, 86, 87,
    88, 116-117
Religion, 20
  belief in mysticism and,
    24
  existence of God and, 20-
    30, 129
  good and evil and, 24-26
  miracles, 24
  morality and, 26-27, 31
  natural selection and, 22
  non-theistic view and, 33-
    38
  sense of duty and, 31-32
  universal design and, 21-
    27
Royce, Josiah, 121

Science, 59
  Aristotelian, 66-67
  causality and, 39-43, 70-
    71, 86-89, 122, 125
  Darwinian, 22, 48, 67-72

Science (*cont.*)
  determinism, 40-44, 75-76, 78
  doctrine of emergence, 74-75
  empirical philosophy and, 62-63
  experimental methods in, 63-64, 74-75
  Galilean, 60, 65-67
  materialism, 76-78
  metaphysical neutrality of, 65-66
  misconceptions in, 59-67
Sense-data, 105, 107, 109, 125
Senses and the Intellect, The (Bain), 15
Septem (social club), 3
Sheldon, David S., 2
Solar system, 34-38
Space, nature of, 90-96
Sparta, 55
Spatial relations, 82, 94-95
Species *see* Natural Selection
Spencer, Herbert, 5, 18, 60, 61, 62
Stephen, Leslie, 9
Sterns, Dr., 118
Stewart, Dugald, 79, 116-117
Substance, concept of, 109-114

Taylor, Miss, 16
Teleology, 67
Tennyson, Alfred Lord, 27-28, 29
Thayer, James Bradley, 1, 3, 11, 56, 57
Theists, 21-27
Thoreau, Henry, 53, 54

Ultimate harmony view, 25-27

Unitarianism, American, 20
Utilitarianism, 44-49, 123, 125
  aesthetic pleasure, 50-52
  moral obligation and, 52-53
  reform and, 53-57
  sensuous pleasure, 50-52
  Francis Wayland on, 52-53

Varieties of Religious Experience, The (James), 128
Vestiges of the Natural History of Creation (Chambers), 2, 17

Walker, Dr., 13
Walker, Mary, 4, 5, 58
Wallace, Alfred Russel, 19
Wayland, Francis, 52-53, 116
Whewell, William, 3
"Will to Believe, The" (James), 129
Winlock, Joseph, 15
Women, rights of, 16, 56
Wright, Ansel, 2
Wright, Chauncey, 1
  a priori knowledge and, 81-85
  American philosophy and, 115, 121, 126
  on arranged marriages, 55
  attitude on Kantian philosophy, 117
  attitudes on creation, 34-38
  background, 1, 2
  characteristics, 1, 2, 4, 5, 7, 8
  common-sense knowledge, 79-81
  concept of cause, 86-89

Wright, Chauncey (*cont.*)
  concept of substance, 109-114
  Charles R. Darwin and, 1, 9-10, 16-19, 67-72, 104
  death of, 10-11
  education, 1, 2-3
  Hamilton and, 12, 16, 90-92, 93-94, 95, 117
  Harvard College and, 1, 2-3, 6, 7, 118-119, 120
  human rights and, 16
  influences on, 1, 2, 3, 9-10, 12, 13-14, 15-16, 17, 59, 121-124
  "Law of the Conditioned" and, 91-92
  morality and, 26-27, 31, 39-58
  nature of space and, 90-96
  non-theistic views and, 33-38
  organized reform and, 53-57
  philosophic contributions of, 126-133
  physical objects, 97-114
  quoted, 7, 8, 32-33, 42-43, 48
  religion and, 20-38
  scientific explanation and, 72-78
  scientific thought and, 59-78
  Scottish philosophy and, 79-80, 116-117
  Socratic philosophy of, 118
  on solar system, 34, 36-38
  Ultimate harmony view, 25-27
  utilitarianism, 44-58
Wright, Elizabeth Boleyn, 2

Zoologists, 22